Peter Eglin and **Stephen Hester**

THE MONTREAL MASSACRE

A Story of Membership Categorization Analysis

Peter Eglin and **Stephen Hester**

THE MONTREAL MASSACRE

A Story of Membership Categorization Analysis

Wilfrid Laurier University Press

WLU

This book has been published with the help of a grant from the Canadian Federation for the Humanities and Social Sciences, through the Aid to Scholarly Publications Programme, using funds provided by the Social Sciences and Humanities Research Council of Canada. We acknowledge the financial support of the Government of Canada through the Book Publishing Industry Development Program for our publishing activities.

National Library of Canada Cataloguing in Publication Data

Eglin, Peter, 1947–
    The Montreal massacre : a story of membership categorization analysis /
Peter Eglin and Stephen Hester.

Includes bibliographical references and index.
ISBN 0-88920-422-5

    1. Montréal École Polytechnique Women Students Massacre, Montréal, Québec, 1989. 2. Crime and the press—Ontario—Case studies. 3. Journalism—Social aspects—Ontario—Case studies. 4. Journalism—Methodology. I. Hester, Stephen, 1947– II. Title.

HV6535.C33M65 2003   070.4'493641523'0820971428   C2003-904094-1

© 2003 Wilfrid Laurier University Press
Waterloo, Ontario, Canada N2L 3C5
www.wlupress.wlu.ca

Cover and text design by P. J. Woodland. Cover image from Cindy McMenemy's assemblage "Daughters Precious Daughters," the artist's response to the Montreal Massacre.

∞
Printed in Canada

Contents

Preface

When Geneviève Bergeron, Hélène Colgan, Nathalie Croteau, Barbara Daigneault, Anne-Marie Edward, Maud Haviernick, Barbara Maria Klucznik, Maryse Laganière, Maryse Leclair, Anne Marie Lemay, Sonia Pelletier, Michèle Richard, Annie St-Arneault, and Annie Turcotte were shot and killed by Marc Lépine on December 6, 1989, it was not as persons with names that they were murdered. They were killed because they were treated as instances of a category: feminists. Indeed, part of the response to the murders consisted of recovering the identities of the victims *as* particular persons with individual lives, rather than as incumbents of a category. Newspapers and other media printed their names, often in a framed or boxed list. Short obituaries were provided of each one. The heartfelt comments of family members were reported as well. We remember the women each year at memorial services on university campuses and elsewhere.

It was initially out of a concern and involvement with gender politics, both on and off campus, that one of us was led to clip the papers as they appeared and to put the clippings in a file. But what brought the clippings out of the file was categories: "You're *women*. You're going to be *engineers*. You're all a bunch of *feminists*." This immediately made the massacre a topic for us given our sociological, that is to say, ethnomethodological, interest in categories. Moreover, the course of action that became formulated as the Montreal Massacre was social-ized from the beginning. That is, in its formulation and execution, and in the reaction to it, it was produced as a societal phenomenon. It was done as and through sociological analysis, both of the lay and more-or-less professional varieties. That included seeing it as having roots in, and consequences for, the social structure itself. Treating the massacre as produced through the sociological analysis of the parties to the event gave it, then, a second relevance for us as ethnomethodologists. For the practices of sociological inquiry form a cardinal, not to say primordial, topic of inquiry for ethnomethodology.

Even though we sought to treat the massacre via our materials as purely a topic of intellectual inquiry, we found it impossible, eight and nine years after the event, not to respond ourselves in more personal ways. Sympathy, sorrow, and anger surfaced (again) as we thought about the victims and their murderer. For us, this posed the question of what to do analytically with our emotions. Moreover, the killer's avowed motive was a political one. He insisted he did it for political reasons, defining his politics in terms of the places and relations of men and women, and giving particular significance to the role of government. Similarly, much of the media commentary we have analyzed addresses at least the first of these selfsame political dimensions. Both of these framings, then, invite their audience to respond politically to them. Where then does our own inquiry stand in relation to such politics? We do not pretend to have satisfactorily answered these questions, but we recognize their seriousness. We have addressed them in the last chapter of this book.

An earlier and summary version of chapters 2, 3, 4, and 5 appears in Paul Jalbert (Ed.), *Media Studies: Ethnomethodological Approaches* (International Institute for Ethnomethodology and Conversation Analysis and University Press of America, 1999). An earlier version of chapter 4 appears in a special issue of *Human Studies* (October 1999), edited by George Psathas and Hisashi Nasu, which contains the papers given at the International Institute for Ethnomethodology and Conversation Analysis International Conference, "Ethnomethodology and Conversation Analysis: East and West," held at Waseda University in Tokyo in August 1997. It also appears in a Japanese translation of selected papers from the conference in *Culture and Society: International Journal of Human Sciences* (October 2000). An earlier version of chapter 6 was presented at the fourteenth annual Qualitative Research Conference, held at the Ontario Institute for Studies in Education of the University of Toronto on August 8, 1997.

We gratefully acknowledge the assistance of Anna Toth and Dorthy Madden, undergraduate students in sociology at Wilfrid Laurier University (WLU) at the time, for assembling and compiling the news clippings into a useable collection of research materials. John McCallum, WLU librarian, was, as usual, timely and helpful in supplying the information on Denis Lortie. The research was supported by a grant partly funded by WLU operating funds and partly from an institutional grant awarded to WLU by the Social Sciences and Humanities Research Council of Canada. We appreciated the support at a later stage of the project given by Rowland Smith, Vice-President: Academic at WLU. We valued the invitation from Colm Kelly of St. Thomas University and Chris Doran of the University of New Brunswick at St. John to present a version of what is now chapter 4 in their Discourse Analysis Research Group Conference Series in Fredericton in March 1997, and the engagement of those present in precisely those questions that we join in chapter 8. We also wish to acknowledge the efforts and contributions of our students in analyzing the phenomena of the Montreal Massacre. We dedicate this work to the special women and girls in our lives, our partners, daughters, and step-daughters, the value of whose presence and contribution is beyond calculation.

INTRODUCTION

CHAPTER 1

Ethnomethodology, Crime, and the Media

▼
INTRODUCTION

THE CRIMES, HORRORS, AND TRAGEDIES of everyday life are endlessly topics of media attention and analysis. In this book we examine media coverage of the homicides that became known as the "Montreal Massacre" in which, on December 6, 1989, at L'École polytechnique in Montreal, gunman Marc Lépine killed fourteen women (thirteen engineering students and a data processing worker), and wounded twelve other people, including some males. Thirteen of the victims had been shot; one was stabbed to death. In one classroom, witnesses reported, the gunman separated the male and female students, ordered the men to leave, and then shot at the women, killing six of them. Just before opening fire, he was reported to have said, "You're all a bunch of feminists. I hate feminists." At the end of his rampage he shot himself dead, leaving a suicide letter explaining his action.

The event occasioned intense media coverage and much commentary. We examined all articles on the subject published in the *Globe and Mail* from Thursday, December 7, to Saturday, December 16, 1989, as well as selected articles in the *Kitchener-Waterloo Record* (as our local paper was then called) over the same period and extending to December 29, 1989.[1] This collection of materials proved sufficient for our purposes, as will become evident below. Furthermore, the last article in our *Globe and Mail* sample itself formulates an ending:

E0   *The self-centred hype of Montreal massacre*
      AT ONE P.M. on Tuesday [Dec 12], Radio-Canada aired its first
      news bulletin in 5-½ days without reference to the massacre of 14
      women students at the Ecole Polytechnique. The murder would
      linger a little longer on open line and public affairs programs. That
      was it, basically, for the bloodiest crime in Quebec's modern history.
      (Dec 16 [1])

Coverage focused on the details of the killings as reported by witnesses (that the killer selected women as his target, what he said, etc.); the response of the police, ambulance service, and coroner's office (what was in the suicide letter he left, a possible second suspect, etc.), the response of government officials (the prime minister, the premier of Quebec, the mayor of Montreal, etc.); the candlelight vigils and funeral/memorial services (who attended, what was said, the number of mourners, etc.); the character and life of the killer (who he was, whether he was insane, whether he was related to any of the victims, his biography, etc.); the response of university and polytechnic officials, engineers, academic experts, gun-shop owners, relatives of the victims, survivors, students, women, and representatives of women's organizations, and so on.

Our approach to these materials is an ethnomethodological one (Garfinkel 1967; Garfinkel and Sacks 1970; Sacks 1992a, 1992b). Our interest, then, is in the Montreal Massacre as a *members' phenomenon*. We will elaborate the significance of this conception later in this chapter when we consider briefly some alternative approaches that have enjoyed sociological and criminological prominence in recent years, namely realism and social constructionism. For now we will confine ourselves to its key point. Thus, to say that we wish to investigate the Montreal Massacre as a members' phenomenon means that we are not offering a theoretical view of it. We do not seek to provide a sociological explanation of the massacre; rather, we aim to discover *what* the Montreal Massacre was as far as the members involved in telling its story were concerned. We are saying that the "facts" of the case—what happened, who the victims were, who the offender was, what kind of event it was, what the motives were, what its consequences were, etc.—are matters for members, and therefore discoverable in their orientations to and treatments of them. Furthermore, insofar as all of these facts were made available in the media coverage— specifically in the media description and analysis contained therein—the Montreal Massacre provides a particularly perspicuous case of how social phenomena are inseparable from and, in a sense, constituted by, the ways in which they are described and analyzed, that is, made accountable in media reportage and commentary.

In researching our materials, we were soon struck by how the emergent phenomena constituting the Montreal Massacre, notably the "problem of violence against women," were dependent on the categories and category predicates used by parties to the event to describe who was involved, what they were doing, and why they were doing it. Our approach, then, is specifically informed by membership categorization analysis (Sacks 1992a; Hester and Eglin 1997a). That is to say, we searched our corpus of media texts both for the categories used to refer to persons and collectivities and for the actions and attributes predicated of them. We then sought to explicate how these category and predicate combinations were constitutive of the news stories and the resultant social phenomena they afforded. Naturally, we recognize that we might have done otherwise and that thereby other organizational aspects of our materials might have been highlighted (cf. Sacks 1992b; Lynch 1993). However, in our view, matters of membership categorization are features of key importance to our phenomenon; without them, it seems to us, the central identifying detail of the phenomena comprising the Montreal Massacre would be lost. They not only provide us with a way of speaking and more than enough to say but are also essential to the story of the Montreal Massacre itself.

In approaching our materials in this way, and mindful of the "Chinese-box" structure of successive accounts of "K" becoming mentally ill (Smith 1978), we became taken up with members' own membership categorization analysis as performed in at least three sorts of accounts in our materials. These are: (1) the newspaper reporters' descriptions (referring to "gunman," "suspect," "students," "witnesses," "police," etc.); (2) the killer's reported speech (for example, "You're all a bunch of feminists," etc.); and (3) the descriptions and formulations employed in the commentaries ("women," "men," "male violence against women," etc.). In the chapters that follow we will take up these accounts in turn, analyzing the methods of membership categorization used by parties in producing the accounts' various constituent phenomena. Our analysis of these phenomena is divided into two major parts. Part 1 contains four chapters in which we are primarily concerned with news stories about the Montreal Massacre as these were made available and organized in and as media reportage. Part 2 contains three chapters in which our focus shifts to the media *commentary* that was developed from the materials provided in the reportage. We conclude the book in chapter 8 with some reflections on our work.

In Part 1, then, and insofar as the primary vehicle of news accounts is the "news story," our first task is that of providing for the production of the stories comprising the Montreal Massacre as a members' phenomenon. The stories themselves may be identified as the crime story, the horror story, the stories of public disaster and private tragedy, the gun-control story, the story of the killer, the killer's story, and the story of violence against women. In chapter 2 we show how categorial resources provide the means by which the massacre's cast of story characters appear, as it were, on cue—and without remark. In chapter 3 we proceed to examine the categorial means that provide for the reportability of the story matters predicated of these characters. Chapter 4 is then devoted to the story told by the killer himself, drawing on one item not fully available at the time of the news coverage we consider, namely, the full text of his suicide letter.

Chapter 5, which bridges Parts 1 and 2, investigates the major story informing the response to and commentary on the massacre: the story of male violence against women. The commentaries that we consider in chapter 5 are taken up with expressing and assessing the meaning and significance of the massacre. This is largely a matter of saying what kind of social problem the killings represent.

In Part 2 chapters 6 and 7 are then devoted to analyzing respectively the explanations that are offered and the consequences that are formulated in the commentaries. In chapter 6 this involves analyzing the use of social context and social structure as explanatory devices, while in chapter 7 it means explicating what we might call "folk functionalism." Since the structural context and functions of deviance are classical subjects of professional sociology, we take the time in these chapters to address such professional sociological accounts in order to show their continuity with lay sociological practices. Finally, in chapter 8, we take up the emotional, ethical, and political questions that pressed themselves on us as we entered into an academic, indeed ethnomethodological, study of our materials.

The organization of our book in this way is not accidental. Rather, it reflects the temporal ordering of the overarching story of the Montreal Massacre itself. Although there are a variety of stories told about the murders, there is also an emergent story that becomes paramount. As reportage is replaced by commentary, so the stories of crime, horror, public disaster, and private tragedy, and the stories of and about the killer, recede, and the story of violence against women becomes the central story.[2] (Later, the story of gun control would take on a life of its own.) Of course, this story of violence against women is based on the inescapable fact that a man shot and killed many women, but the subsequent story this engenders is not just about the particular event. As reportage gives way to commentary (though we emphasize that there is no clean or tidy break here), so particularity becomes the document of a general and underlying problem, namely, male violence against women, not to say misogyny or male chauvinism. We seek to trace the accomplishment of this story, principally in the methods of membership categorization deployed by its storytellers. There is, furthermore, a pervasive irony here. Just as the killer grounded his actions in his categorization of his victims, so is a similar categorial logic displayed in the story based upon them.

In the remainder of this opening chapter, we outline the nature of an ethnomethodological approach to crime and the media, distinguishing it from realist and social constructionist approaches, and we give a brief synopsis of membership categorization analysis.

▼
ETHNOMETHODOLOGY, CRIME, AND THE MEDIA

As an ethnomethodological study, this book offers an alternative to the approaches of realism and social constructionism, which have traditionally bifurcated the sociology of crime and deviance (Maynard 1988). Such bifurcation obscures characteristics that these traditions share with each other: theoreticism and ironicism. In both realism and social constructionism, the standard sociological practice of distinguishing the analyst (theorist) and the (ordinary) member of society permits the analyst to say what crime and deviance *are* and what their significance is quite independent of members' orientations. The realist, for example, on the basis of an objective definition of crime, can argue not only that there is a "dark figure of crime" which is much greater than that contained in official counts but also that the public's fears and estimates of crime are incorrect—that is, they do not correspond to an independent reality of crime. Common-sense conceptions of crime are denigrated as *mis*conceptions. Similarly, the social constructionist, on the premise that crime *is* a social construction, can argue that what are oriented to as "facts" (for example, crime rates are rising or falling, certain types and instances of behaviour are deviant or criminal) are *in actual fact* ideological fictions, socially constructed *artefacts* of, for example, the application of interpretations, definitions, and judgements, the use of assumptions about the reality of crime and guilt and innocence thereof, and the various claims-making activities in and through which conceptions of crime are articulated and eventually sedimented in moral and legal structures.

In terms of these approaches, our materials might have been deployed in various ways. A realist analysis could have involved the inspection of the materials for clues regarding the antecedents and determinants of the massacre as a form of behaviour, perhaps with respect to other instances of mass murder and serial killing. Similarly, the murders might reasonably provide for attempts to measure the level and distribution of different kinds of female victimization and to make ameliorative and correctional recommendations thereto. In a social constructionist investigation, on the other hand, our materials could have been inspected in terms of the question of the role of the media in the social construction of the problem of violence against women. Since our interest is an ethnomethodological one, we have pursued neither of these particular avenues of inquiry here for reasons that we will now seek to explain.

As Maynard (1988) indicates, ethnomethodology, and specifically the analysis of talk in interaction, provides a means of transcending the realist/social constructionist bifurcation. Maynard emphasizes the pivotal role of language and social interaction with respect to *any* theoretical specification of the social processes constitutive of crime and deviance. While we would endorse this emphasis, our take on realism and social constructionism derives from a rather different premise. For us, in contrast to *both* realism and social constructionism, ethnomethodology neither theorizes nor ironicizes members' social activities. As we have indicated elsewhere (Hester and Eglin 1997b: 1), "ethnomethodology (EM) is, above all else, a policy towards inquiry, an analytic mentality, that insists on (1) doing studies, by (2) working on materials to see what can be discovered in and from them, rather than selecting problems and data on the basis of some theoretically-specified agenda (Sharrock and Watson 1989: 434–435)." Consequently, while for realism and social constructionism the nature of crime and deviance is a matter of theoretical debate, for ethnomethodology they are not matters about which any *theoretical stance* needs to be or should be taken (cf. Hester and Francis 1997). Accordingly, then, the problematics for realism and social constructionism are eschewed at the outset. Instead, because it examines crime and deviance as *members' phenomena,* ethnomethodology seeks to analyze and describe the ways in which concerns with crime and deviance inform members' locally ordered practical action and practical reasoning; its aim is to describe the mundane practices in and through which persons are oriented to issues of what is criminal (or deviant) and engage in its analysis in the course of such activities as reporting, describing, questioning, interpreting, deciding, explaining, and formulating the consequences of what is or is not deviant. If there is analysis to be done, it is analysis of, and grounded in, members' analysis.

One consequence of ethnomethodology's focus on crime and deviance as irremediably a members' phenomenon is that sociological theorizing about crime and deviance is respecified as a species of members' practical action and practical reasoning. The distinction between analyst (theorist) and member is collapsed in the sense that the privilege accorded to professional sociological (or criminological) theories is removed, and it is recognized that just as professional sociologists theorize about *how* or *why* persons come to be deviant, so also do ordinary members of society. Accordingly, it is unsurprising that both realism and social constructionism (and other sociological and criminological approaches) may not turn up in another guise, that is, as members' phenomena, as indeed they do in our materials, as we indicate in chapters 5, 6, and 7.

Likewise, from our point of view, we do not seek to interpret the media in terms of a pre-formulated theory of their role in relation to gender, crime, or anything else. For several decades now, the media have been cast as players in such sociological dramas as the creation of moral panics, the construction of social problems, and the perpetuation of inequality and oppression. These sociological language games (Bogen and Lynch 1993) have embodied a privileging of the sociological theorist's viewpoint and a corresponding disinterest in the organization of social life *from within.* The order of things is accessible only through the conceptual machinery of sociological theory. Natural language use and social interaction become transformed into resources for the construction of sociological accounts. In contrast, we do not seek to find evidence of *any* particular theory of the media. Rather, our interest is only in ethnomethodological aspects of the media (Jalbert 1999).[3] Accordingly, we seek to discover the cultural and organizational structures, that is to say, the *methodical* structures in, and through which, media phenomena are accomplished.

We realize, of course, that our analysis pertains only to media *texts,* to what might be understood as the residue of all that practical and interactional work that has gone into the production of those texts. We understand therefore that we might have investigated other organized aspects of the work of newspaper reportage and commentary. However, we are not deluded thereby to conclude that a complete picture could otherwise have been provided, nor that the inevitable partiality of our account requires supplementation or, for that matter, triangulation. Rather, as we have contended and sought to show elsewhere (Eglin and Hester 1992; Hester and Eglin 1992, 1997c; cf. Lee 1984), it is our view that there is much to be gained from an inspection of the detail of media texts *in themselves.*

▼
MEMBERSHIP CATEGORIZATION ANALYSIS

We have elsewhere (Eglin and Hester 1992, Hester and Eglin 1997b) outlined the main features and history of membership categorization analysis, and so we will not repeat ourselves unduly at this juncture. However, some explication is in order, not least for those who may be otherwise unfamiliar with this particular approach within the ethnomethodological corpus.[4]

In a series of brilliant studies, Harvey Sacks discovered, investigated, and developed a domain of inquiry whose central focus was on the uses of membership categorization devices, membership categories, category predicates, and associated rules and maxims in talk, especially conversation. Some of these studies were published separately, but most of them remained in the form of lectures and research notebooks that did not appear until *Lectures on Conversation* was published in 1992, seventeen years after his death. In line with his general interest in the objects that people use to accomplish social activities, Sacks sought to show how categorizational phenomena comprised a machinery or apparatus for understanding and achieving conversational interaction. An early example consisted of identifying just those categorial resources of which the use and analytic depiction would "reproduce" the conclusion that a suicidal person might reach, namely, that they had "no one to turn to." Likewise, in the most famous example of work in this genre, Sacks described the categorial apparatus used to find a sense of the children's story "the baby cried, the mommy picked it up." It was here that Sacks laid out the key steps followed in much membership categorization analysis: find or make one's common sense of some piece of talk or text, and then turn that sense into an object of investigation. The aim of analysis is to identify *how* sense is achieved.

Of course, categories and the collections that they compose, together with associated phenomena such as viewer's, hearer's, and doer's maxims, may be used to accomplish a much wider range of activities than making sense alone. As studies by Schegloff (1972), Watson (1978, 1983, 1990), Drew (1978), and Jayyusi (1984), amongst others, as well as by Sacks himself, have shown, categories are interactionally deployable in formulating locations, doing accusations, making excuses, allocating blame, finding a motive, telling a story, and so on. It is just such interactional uses of categories, albeit textually achieved, that we are at pains to discover and reveal in the analysis that makes up our study here.

▼
CONCLUDING REMARKS

In the chapters that follow, then, membership categorization analysis affords an investigation into two main topics. First, it permits us to analyze and describe the categorial organization of the various stories comprising the reportage and commentary on, and the killer's own version of, the Montreal Massacre. Second, it allows us not only to examine the central organizational resources deployed in the telling of these stories, it also affords an insight into how the phenomenon that came to be known as the Montreal Massacre was constituted through this "production-recognition" apparatus. In our conclusion, we show how our approach may also provide a way of addressing some of the emotional, political, and ethical issues, not least for us, that were touched off by the murders and their media coverage (see Malette and Chalouh 1991; Fahmy 1994).

PART 1

Stories of the Montreal Massacre

CHAPTER 2

The Story Characters Appear on Cue

▼
INTRODUCTION

BEFORE TURNING OUR ATTENTION in chapter 3 to the various stories that make up the Montreal Massacre as an accountable phenomenon, we want to begin here by providing for *who* turns up in these stories. In doing so we wish to note that—and how—these persons comprise an *unremarkable* collection of story characters. We will argue that the selection and identification of these persons is generated from the categorial resources made available by the initial characterization of the event. Our inspiration here is the following remarkable passage from Sacks's lectures in which he introduces the idea that "character appears on cue."

> Now we'll say that for some pairs of activities, pairs of actions that are related by norms, that there's at least a rule of adequate description which says "character appears on cue," i.e., if the first takes place and it's an adequate grounds for the second taking place, then it's okay to describe the thing without having provided for how it is that that second person happened to come on the scene to do whatever it is they properly do, if one says the first occurs and the second occurs as well. (Sacks 1992a: 254)

Since our argument turns on the significance of the initial characterization, we will start by considering the *Globe and Mail*'s first story, which appeared on the front page on Thursday, December 7, the morning after the massacre:

E1   **MAN IN MONTREAL KILLS 14 WITH RIFLE**
Canadian Press and Staff
MONTREAL
A gunman went on a rampage at the University of Montreal last night, killing 14 people before shooting himself dead.

Police took away a second suspect in handcuffs an hour after the shootings began. Late last night, a heavily armed police tactical team was combing the six-storey engineering building of the Ecole Polytechnique, which is affiliated with the university, for a possible third suspect.

Claude St. Laurent, a spokesman for the Montreal police, said the man taken away in handcuffs was being questioned. Some students said they recognized the man as a part-time physics teacher, but police would not confirm that or release his name.

Police also would not release the name of the gunman or any of the 14 other dead people.

Earlier, a spokesman for the Urgence-Sante, the Montreal ambulance service, said at least 12 people were injured.

Witnesses said two and perhaps three men—one of them carrying a hunting rifle—burst into a crowded computer class about 5:30 p.m., shouting anti-feminist slogans.

"He (the man with the gun) ordered the men and women to separate sides of the classroom," said Louis Hamel, 24, a second-year engineering student.

"We thought it was a joke, then the man fired a shot, and all hell broke loose."

Witnesses said the young gunman, who spoke French, roamed the halls and classrooms of the university's engineering building, shooting students on at least two floors.

The building, which can hold up to 5,000 students, was evacuated and sealed off by police shortly after the shooting began.

"I saw death close up and I shook," said Vanthona Ouy, 22, one of scores of horrified students who streamed out of the building.

"All I know is that a crazy guy came in here and began shooting at anything that moved," said Dominique Berube, 22. "It's our friends who have been killed."

There were reports that the gunman shot mainly women students, but police would not release a breakdown of victims by gender.

Francois Bordeleau, a student, ran from the first to the second floor and dragged people by the collar to keep them from going in the man's direction.

"It was a human hunt," he said. "We were the quarry."

He said he heard 20 to 30 shots and the man appeared to be aiming mainly at women. "I heard the gunman say: 'I want the women,'" Mr. Bordeleau said. That was confirmed by several other witnesses.

Witnesses said the gunman entered several rooms including the computer room and the building cafeteria.

In the computer room, he aimed at the wall and then ran out, said Lucien Justin, who was in the room. "Somebody locked the door, but he shot off the lock and then left a second time.

"I was terribly afraid, I ran like hell," Mr. Justin said.

At least 20 ambulances were on the scene, taking the wounded to four hospitals in the area. (Dec 7 [1])

▼

OFFENDERS, EMERGENCIES, AND DEATHS: THE CRIME STORY AND ITS ADJUNCTS

The headline provides the news content of the story; it's a mass homicide. The event may be said to implicate an initial pair of categories for describing the parties, namely "offender" and "victim(s)." These may be said to constitute a standardized relational pair in relation to a potentially criminal act such as homicide (Watson 1983; Hester and Eglin 1992: chap. 6). As such, they provide for the relevance of others' actions and for their own transformation into other categories in the context of those others' actions. Sacks continues:

> but if the first is, for example a violation, then you can provide that the second occurred. For example, "he was speeding and he got arrested." Perfectly okay...What occurs is good grounds for the cop to do what he ought to do; he's on the scene and he does it. So he's introduced via the action he does, where the grounds for that action are laid out, though how he happens to be there need not be indicated. (1992a: 254,183)

Thus the homicides reported in the headline and in the first sentence of the news story become the motive for the involvement of the police, and thereby the appearance of the police on cue, and without explanation of how they got there, in the second sentence of the story. Thus:

E2   A gunman went on a rampage at the University of Montreal last
       night, killing 14 people before shooting himself dead.
           Police took away a second suspect in handcuffs an hour after
       the shootings began. (Dec 7 [1]; emphasis added)

To spell it out, the reader understands that the police action reported in the second sentence is in response to the killings reported in the first sentence (and not some other story concerned with other shootings). This is made possible by the reader invoking the rule "character appears on cue." The idea expressed in the phrase "character appears on cue" was reconceptualized by Sacks in his published analysis of "The baby cried" as the "second viewer's maxim": "If one sees a pair of actions which can be related via the operation of a norm that provides for the second given the first, where the doers can be seen as members of the categories the norm provides as proper for that pair of actions, then (a) see that the doers are such-members, and (b) see the second as done in conformity with the norm" (Sacks 1974: 225).

Throughout the story "Man in Montreal Kills 14 with Rifle" (pp. 13–15), and in subsequent news stories, the same means provide for transforming the offender ("gunman") into "[murder] suspect" and "killer," and others present into "witnesses." Witnesses, for example, appear unannounced in the eighth sentence. These categories, including "victims," may be said to form the collection "parties to an offence" (Watson 1983: 36). To these categories are tied a number of predicated activities, such as the police arresting and questioning suspects (second and fourth sentences), searching for other possible suspects (third sentence), releasing the names of offender, suspects, and victims (fifth and sixth sentences), trying to determine the killer's motive, and appealing for other witnesses (subsequent articles). Specifying Watson's title, let us call the combination of categories-from-the-collection and their tied predicates the membership categorization device "PHI" (parties to a homicide investigation). Using it as an interpretive scheme permits the reader to find the relevance in, and see the connectedness of, not only the first six sentences of narrative in Extract 1 considered above but also of a sequence of reported speech, such as that contained in the following news report:

E3   *Killer fraternized with men in army fatigues*

Marc Lepine, who killed 14 women and wounded 12 other people in a shooting rampage at the University of Montreal on Wednesday, hung out with a small band of men who walked around their neighborhood wearing army fatigues.

Employees at a grocery store across the street from the killer's flat on a narrow street just east of the downtown core said yesterday that Mr. Lepine and his friends rented war and violent action films from a nearby video store.

"They loved watching army and violent films," *one employee* said...

Another employee said Mr. Lepine would sometimes make caustic comments about women...

At a *nearby camping and hunting supply store, a clerk* said Mr. Lepine was a frequent visitor...

...

Claude Boilly, director of the CEGEP, said teachers vaguely remember Mr. Lepine.

...

Major Serge Quenneville, a spokesman for the Canadian Forces in Montreal, confirmed that Mr. Lepine had applied in the winter of 1980–81 under his former name and was rejected.

...

Neighbours said he shared a $285-a-month, five-room, second floor flat with a young, blond man named Eric.

...

Maurice Dutrisac, his landlord, said he was shocked to learn that Mr. Lepine had committed the murders. (Dec 9 [3]; emphasis added)

That is, the appearance in the story of assorted persons identified as "employees at a grocery store across the street from the killer's flat," "one employee," "another employee," "a clerk [at a] nearby camping and hunting supply store," "Claude Boilly, director of the CEGEP," "Major Serge Quenneville, a spokesman for the Canadian Forces in Montreal," "neighbours," and "Maurice Dutrisac, his landlord," makes sense as a motivated collection of persons under the auspices of "character appears on cue," where PHI provides for their identifiability as "witnesses" or "persons with information potentially relevant to this homicide investigation." The same means repair the indexicality of all such expressions (including also "the killer," "nearby," "Mr. Lépine," and "he"). Furthermore, PHI is the initial formal basis for developing one theme in the crime story into a story in its own right, what we call in chapter 3 "the story of the killer."

The telling of the stories comprising the Montreal Massacre as a members' phenomenon is carried on not only in the reporting of events and of witnesses' reports of events, but also in the response to and commentary on those events by "third parties." The selection of commentators is organized, then, in categorial terms and conducted in terms of category relevance, where for features of the homicides a collection of relevant categories of commentators is a touched off matter. That is, in terms of "character appears on cue," those who comment are an unsurprising collection whose selection does not have to be provided for other than in categorial terms. Yet the very unremarkability of those who comment, and of the comments they make, belies formal organizational considerations pertaining to the selection of *these* resources for telling the news. Thus, if the event is an X, then select Y (but not Z) as a commentator for quotation; similarly, if the victim is an X, then Y (but not Z) as a comment. These formal considerations can be said to "organize" the story of the Montreal Massacre. Thus, insofar as the homicides are constituted as "crime," that is, as murders— indeed a mass murder—then categories of commentator for whom commenting about crime is a recognizable predicate can be expected to, and indeed unremarkably do, appear on cue: sociologists, criminologists, anthropologists, psychologists, persons who have written books about mass murderers, murder experts, and other characters with a special interest or skill on issues such as criminal motivation and the causes of crime are used to address topics touched off by the crime. For example:

E4 "This is perhaps the first crime perpetrated against a whole sex. That's what this is all about," said University of Montreal *criminologist,* Jean-Paul Brodeur. (Dec 8 [2]; emphasis added)

E5   Before the mid-1960s, mass murders were very few. *Criminologist*
      James Fox of Boston's Northeastern University says there now are
      30 a year in the United States.
      ...
      Dr. Lana Stermac, a senior *psychologist* at Toronto's Clarke Institute
      of Psychiatry, said she and her colleagues could recall no precedent
      of such a systematic sorting out of people as Mr. Lepine did in the
      engineering classroom. (Dec 8 [6]; emphasis added)

E6   **Mass murders not increasing, Canadian *anthropologist* says**
      The phenomenon of mass murder is still a relatively obscure crime
      in Canada, says the country's leading expert in the field.
          Elliot Leyton, an *anthropologist* at Memorial University in New-
      foundland, says the senseless slaying of 14 women at the Univer-
      sity of Montreal on Wednesday, combined with the recent murders
      of four people in northeastern New Brunswick, creates the impres-
      sion that multiple killings are on the increase.
          That is not the case, he said. (Dec 8 [10]; emphasis added)

To return to the first news report of the massacre, Extract 1, we have noted
that after the opening sentence the next five sentences are devoted to telling the
crime story; police figure in each one of these sentences. They may be said to
be generated out of the resources of PHI, itself made available in the headline
and first sentence. But the seventh sentence ("Earlier..."; see E7 below) has a
different pair of actors, "people [who] were injured" and (the organizational
actor) "the Montreal ambulance service." Yet the character who appears, namely
"a spokesman" for the organization, may be said to have been cued in the first
sentence (and again in the sixth sentence). Killings transform "victims" into
"dead" and "injured" or "wounded" people who, as *medical emergencies,*
become the business of ambulance services and paramedics (and subsequently
of doctors, nurses, and surgeons), who also arrive in the story on cue. From
Extract 1:

E7   Police also would not release the name of the gunman or any of
      the 14 other dead people.
          Earlier, a spokesman for *the Urgence-Sante, the Montreal ambu-
      lance service,* said at least 12 people were injured. (Dec 7 [1];
      emphasis added)

E8   "I was terribly afraid, I ran like hell," Mr. Justin said.
          At least 20 *ambulances* were on the scene, taking the wounded
      to four hospitals in the area. (Dec 7 [1]; emphasis added)

In E7 "dead people" can be read as both invoking the category "victim" from the
"offender/victim" relational pair, *and* the category "dead and wounded" from

the pair in which the other category is, say, "emergency service" (such as ambulance service). In this way the appearance of these categorial objects is accountably in accordance with the norm that provides for their relationship and as such needs no explanation; such absent explanations are not seen as missing.

Similarly, homicides are a class of *medico-legal events* where "victims" become co-terminous with their names, sexes, and ages; they are civic objects to be officially identified and accounted for. As such they become part of the workload of coroners:

E9   At the news conference, *Chief Coroner* Jean Grenier said all the victims have been identified and the families have been advised. Then, to a hushed room, he read the names and ages of the 14 dead women. He said autopsies were being carried out. (Dec 8 [1]; emphasis added)

▼
THE UNIVERSITY AND ITS CATEGORIES: THE HORROR STORY

Formulations of the *setting* are themselves category-generative. The headline of the first story (E1 above) locates the event in "Montreal." The first sentence of the article specifies the setting as the "University of Montreal." The third sentence refers to "the six-storey engineering building of the Ecole Polytechnique, which is affiliated with the university." In the eighth sentence "a crowded computer class" is introduced. Subsequently, reference is made to "the classroom," "the halls and classrooms of the university's engineering building," "the building," "two floors," "the first to the second floor," the "building cafeteria" and "the computer room." This sequence of place formulations itself provides a nice example of the use of a "common-sense geography"—that of a university campus—to organize the telling of the story (see Sacks 1986; Schegloff 1972; Drew 1978; McHoul and Watson 1984; Eglin and Hester 1992: 249–250, 263; Hester and Eglin 1997b: 9-11). However, our point here is to bring out how the place formulations, from the "University of Montreal" on, provide for the relevance of identifying persons at the scene in terms of the hearably co-selected, university-campus categories of "students," "teacher," "professor," "faculty," "dean," "president," "students association" and so on. Moreover, like the membership categorization devices "family" and "baseball team," the collection "university personnel" appears to have the property of "duplicative organization" (Sacks 1974). That is, not only does this setting-based collection provide, via the consistency rule, for readers to see that these are *university* students and teachers (and not, say, their primary or secondary school equivalents), readers may take it that these are students and teachers at one and the same university, *this* university, the University of Montreal. Thus, from Extract 1:

E10   Claude St. Laurent, a spokesman for the Montreal police, said the man taken away in handcuffs was being questioned. Some *students* said they recognized the man as a *part-time physics teacher.* (Dec 7 [1]; emphasis added)

E11 Witnesses said two and perhaps three men—one of them carrying a hunting rifle—burst into a crowded computer class about 5:30 p.m., shouting anti-feminist slogans.

   "He (the man with the gun) ordered the men and women to separate sides of the classroom," said Louis Hamel, 24, *a second-year engineering student.* (Dec 7 [1]; emphasis added)

That is, once again, the unexplained appearance of "students" in the fifth sentence of the opening article (after four sentences of police action) is the appearance of a class of characters cued from the first sentence by the description of the scene in terms of a "relevant category environment" (Jayyusi 1984: 135) founded in the initial characterization of the setting as a "university." In chapter 3 we shall argue that the description of the setting in terms of the categories and category-tied activities "belonging" to a university campus is a crucial resource for the making of a horror story out of the events of the massacre. Here, however, our purpose is, to repeat, to provide for who it is who turns up in these stories. To return to the cases at hand, readers may have recourse to the same device to find the identity of the "students" referred to in the headline of the second story on the first day of coverage, appearing on page five:

E12 Terrified *students* describe shooting scene. (Dec 7 [2]; emphasis added)

Some further examples follow:

E13 Still in shock after the massacre at the Ecole Polytechnique late Wednesday afternoon, teary-eyed *students and members of the faculty* huddled in the lobby of the school recounting the ordeal and mourning their friends.

   ...

   Helene David, *psychology professor* at the University of Montreal, urged anyone traumatized by the tragic event to seek help as soon as possible.

   ...

   "This is perhaps the first crime perpetrated against a whole sex. That's what this is all about," said *University of Montreal criminologist,* Jean-Paul Brodeur. (Dec 8 [2]; emphasis added)

E14 It does not appear to be coincidence that Mr. Lepine chose the engineering school, one of life's remaining male enclaves being entered by women. ("What do I say to the parents," asked Louis Courville, *dean of the engineering school,* his voice breaking with emotion. "They send us their daughters who are then killed.") (Dec 8 [6]; emphasis added)

E15   "Our 14 sisters from Polytechnique cannot be replaced, but it is essential that the whole community of engineers unite so that other women may take over in this profession," *the students association* said in a news release. (Dec 11 [1]; emphasis added)

E16   The *Ontario Confederation of University Faculty Associations* is shocked and saddened by the tragedy at the Ecole Polytechnique, University of Montreal. The symbolism of singling out and executing 14 women studying in a *professional higher education faculty* cannot be lost on those who are concerned about the violence against and control of women in our culture. (Dec 11 [2]; emphasis added)

▼
PUBLIC DISASTER AND PERSONAL TRAGEDY

The scale, reportability, and associated characteristics of the massacre make of it a tragic public event, indeed a *public disaster.* As such it comes under the purview of public officials, that is, the political leaders — the mayor, the provincial premier, the relevant cabinet minister, the prime minister—who appear on cue in the second day's reporting:

E17   **Quebec mourns senseless deaths**
Flags were flying at half-staff across the province yesterday as Quebeckers tried to come to terms with a man's senseless killing of 14 young women who wanted to become engineers.

Still in shock after the massacre at the Ecole Polytechnique late Wednesday afternoon, teary-eyed students and members of the faculty huddled in the lobby of the school recounting the ordeal and mourning their friends.
...

The *Quebec National Assembly* observed a minute of silence and *Premier Robert Bourassa* declared a three-day period of official mourning. University officials have approached the parents of the victims and offered to help organize joint funeral services on Monday, but plans have not yet been finalized.

Last night, almost 5,000 people braved sub-zero temperatures to participate in a candlelight vigil to mourn the loss of students and friends. Escorted by police officers, they made their way in solemn silence to the Ecole Polytechnique on the slopes of Mount Royal.

> *Prime Minister Brian Mulroney and his wife, Mila,* arrived at the Ecole Polytechnique to pay their respects last night...
> ...
>
> "December 6th will be among the blackest days in Montreal's history. The population is in a state of shock and the pain won't disappear in a couple of days," *Montreal Mayor Jean Dore* said. (Dec 8 [2]; emphasis added)

We take up the question of the "constitutive accent" the massacre-as-a-public-disaster gives to our materials in chapter 7.

But as *tragic personal events,* homicides (like suicides and accidental deaths) invoke the relevance of "R," the collection of standardized relational pairs relevant to the search for help (Sacks 1972).[1] Such category pairs are "husband-wife," "parent-child," "friend-friend," "neighbour-neighbour," and so on. Under the auspices of R, the deaths of the victims become events in the lives of friends and relatives. "Victims" become transformed as "friends," "daughters," "wives," "girlfriends," each category invoking its other pair-part, "friends," "parents (mother, father)," "husbands," "boyfriends (girlfriends)." Thus, in Extract 17 above, reference is made to the dead victims as "friends" (second and sixth sentences) and to their "parents" (fifth sentence). It is not necessary to explain who the friends are who are being referred to, nor why university officials should seek to offer assistance to parents of victims. Reference to these characters is explicable by R. Indeed, there is a case already in Extract 1:

E18   "It's our *friends* who have been killed." (Dec 7 [1]; emphasis added)

Furthermore:

E19   **OUR *DAUGHTERS,* OURSELVES**
They are so precious to us, our daughters.
...

So now our daughters are truly frightened and it makes their mothers furious that they are frightened. (Dec 9 [5]; emphasis added)

E20   Croteau's *father* weeps over her coffin yesterday in Montreal [photo caption]. (*Globe and Mail,* Dec 11 [A1]; emphasis added)

E21   Families, friends remember victims' lives. (Dec 11 [5]; emphasis added)

And so on.

TRAGIC MASS MURDERS AND POLITICIANS: THE GUN CONTROL STORY

Also appearing on the second day of news coverage are "opposition members of parliament" and "the government" and their respective representatives:

E22 *Opposition MPs* **demand long-promised gun control**

Opposition members of Parliament urged the *government* yesterday to bring forward long-promised legislation to amend Canada's gun control laws in the wake of the tragic mass murders in Montreal on Wednesday.

"We've been waiting for over three years now," *New Democrat Svend Robinson* told reporters.

...

Justice Minister Douglas Lewis would not say when the government's initiative to restrict automatic weapons would be brought before the House, only that it would be "as soon as possible."

But the *government* has no plans to ban the type of weapon used in the Montreal killings. The killer, identified by police as Marc Lepine, used a semi-automatic rifle made by Sturm, Ruger and Co. in Southport, Conn. (Dec 8 [8]; emphasis added)

The weapon used in the killings is reported in the headline and first sentence of the first news story on the first day: the killing was done "with [a] rifle;" the killer is a "gunman" (see E1 above). Given "the tragic mass murders" (E22, first sentence) carried out by a gunman with a rifle, it is not surprising when characters drawn from the pair of categories "government/opposition" appear in the story. Indeed their appearance touches off a new story, that of the political issue of gun control.

OFFENDER AND VICTIMS: THE KILLER'S STORY AND THAT OF VIOLENCE AGAINST WOMEN

Again, in the first news article on the first day, other categories (than those we have considered so far) are used that cue the appearance of further tied categories later in the story. Thus, the killer is reported by witnesses to have selected his victims and to have made his own categorizations of them. From Extract 1:

E23 "He (the man with the gun) ordered the *men and women* to separate sides of the classroom."

...

There were reports that the gunman shot mainly *women students*, but police would not release a breakdown of victims by gender.

...

> He said he heard 20 to 30 shots and the man appeared to be aim-
> ing mainly at *women*. "I heard the gunman say: 'I want the *women*,'"
> Mr. Bordeleau said. (Dec 7 [1]; emphasis added)

The equivalent story in the *Kitchener-Waterloo Record* includes the following paragraph (and also highlights the killer's words in a separate box):

E24   One student said the gunman threatened his cornered victims,
shouting: "'You're *women*. You're going to be *engineers*. You're all
a bunch of *feminists*. I hate *feminists*!'" (*KWR*, Dec 7 [1]; emphasis added)

These categorizations are the formal basis for the telling both of what we call
"the killer's story" (see chapter 4) and "the story of violence against women"
(see chapter 5). Here our point is to note how they provide further cues for further characters to appear. Thus, the killer's description of his victims as "women,"
"engineers," and "feminists" makes relevant the responses of those who are
co-incumbents of these categories. For example, from reaction reported on
the second day:

E25   "As *women* we feel a deep, deep remorse that we can't bring these
(14) women back, said Charlene Nero, one of the co-ordinators of
last night's candlelight vigil.
...
"The event did not happen in a vacuum," said Ms Nero, a spokesman for the *Committee de Defence des Femmes*, a group created
in the wake of last year's rape of a young woman at a McGill University fraternity. (Dec 8 [2]; emphasis added)

E26   ***Hundreds in Toronto mourn killing of 14 women***
They [mourners] were horrified when Alice de Wolff, a Toronto organizer for the *National Action Committee on the Status of Women*,
told them...
...
"Women live with violence on a day to day basis just because we're
women," said Mavis Wilson, the *cabinet minister responsible for
women's issues in the Ontario government.*
...
Toronto lawyer Mary Lou McPhedran, who organized the service
with the help of *well-known feminists* like Nancy Jackman and Linda
Nye, said the same thing to the crowd. (Dec 8 [7]; emphasis added)

And in subsequent days' coverage:

E27   Meanwhile, a spokesman for the *Quebec Corporation of Engineers* said women engineers throughout Canada will wear a white scarf Monday to "mark their solidarity with the slain engineering students."

The idea was launched Thursday by *Montreal engineer* Micheline Bouchard and quickly picked up by a *nation-wide network of women engineers*. (Dec 9 [1]; emphasis added)

E28   *Quebec engineers* observe day of mourning. (Dec 12 [4]; emphasis added)

E29   **"Men cannot know the feelings of fear"**
        Yet an anti-feminist backlash has been intensified
                by the massacre in Montreal
                BY MELANIE RANDALL

Ms Randall is a doctoral student in political science at York University and a *researcher-activist in the field of women and violence*. (Dec 12 [2]; emphasis added to "researcher-activist...")

That is, it is unsurprising that the report that Lépine not only murdered women who were student-engineers but also addressed his victims as "women," "engineers," and "feminists" should make relevant and therefore provide for the appearance of co-incumbents of these categories as commentators. They become relevant by virtue not of the fact that they are known to or are related to them (for example, as family members) but because there are categorial connections between the victims as occupants of the categories "women," "engineers," and "feminists" (so called) and the commentators as co-incumbents of these categories or as spokespersons for the incumbents of them. Accordingly, in addition to professional journalists and columnists, commentators and those quoted were drawn from categories such as "Quebec Corporation of Engineers," "well-known feminists," "feminist writer," "spokespersons for women's organizations," "researcher-activist in the field of women and violence," "spokesperson for pro-feminist men's organizations," "university officials/cabinet ministers responsible for women's issues," and so forth. We give detailed attention to these commentaries in chapter 5.

▼
CONCLUSION

The categories and category pairs, together with their category-tied activities (Turner 1970; Jayyusi 1984: 37) and other predicates that we have reviewed in this chapter, provide, then, some of the procedural resources that newspaper and news readers may use to produce and recognize respectively the relevance of the variety of actors and actions that appear in the text of the articles. Where the articles deal with the crime story and what becomes the story of the killer, we are quoted police and various categories of witness. Where the articles relate the horror story or the tragedy, we get "one of scores of horrified students who streamed out of the building" (Dec 7 [1]), "terrified students [who] describe shooting scene" (Dec 7 [2]), "still in shock…teary-eyed students and members of the faculty" (Dec 8 [2]), "parents of some of the young women who died in the massacre [who] expressed shock and horror" (Dec 8 [9]), and "weeping and holding one another for comfort, hundreds of women and men—most of them students, professors, politicians and community activists" (Dec 8 [7]). Where the story is that of gun control, we get in the first place the category pair "government/opposition." Where the articles engage in commentary on the scope, explanation, and significance of the problem, notably the problem of violence against women, it is provided by persons referred to in terms of political, academic, or other organizational (women's, engineering…) categories.

Finally, and in anticipation of a topic we take up in the next chapter, let us note how "character appears on cue" can be a formal basis for the occurrence of tragedy. Two matters deemed newsworthy enough to report turn on characters appearing on cue who subsequently find they stand in a second relationship to the event by virtue of a further category incumbency they hold. Particular note is made of, and special treatment accorded to, persons who cross over categories, for this is one definition of "news."

E30   "December 6th will be among the blackest days in Montreal's history. The population is in a state of shock and the pain won't disappear in a couple of days," *Montreal Mayor* Jean Dore said…

        Mr. Dore, wiping tears away, said one of the victims was the *daughter of a friend* and had been his own *daughter's babysitter.* (Dec 8 [2]; emphasis added)

E31   Maryse Leclair, 23-year-old *daughter* of the *director of public relations for the Montreal police,* was stabbed with a hunting knife found on the floor beside her body, Andre Tessier, head of the force's organized crime squad, confirmed yesterday.

        Pierre Leclair discovered his *daughter* lying dead on the floor when he entered the building after answering reporters' questions outside. (Dec 11 [1]; emphasis added; see also Dec 8 [9])

That is, in Extract 30, Jean Doré is both the "Montreal Mayor" and as such an official commentator on the massacre; at the same time he is the friend of the father of one of the victims who was herself babysitter to his own daughter. In Extract 31, the "director of public relations for the Montreal police," at the scene in his occupational capacity, is also "Pierre Leclair," the "devastated" (Dec 8 [9]) father of one of the victims. The *Kitchener-Waterloo Record* devotes, indeed, a small article to the gruesome discovery: "Policeman finds body of daughter" (*KWR,* Dec 7 [4]).

In this way, then, under the auspices of "character appears on cue" these categories and predicates provide for the coherence of juxtaposed and sequentially organized discrete items of information as they turn up in the reportage. They provide, that is, for the story of the Montreal Massacre itself, in two senses of news story—that is, the sense in which the expression may be used to refer to a particular bounded textual item, a particular news report, and that in which it may be used to refer to one or other ongoing story being told in such reports and in associated commentary. For with these resources the newspaper may produce an elaborate skein of actual stories, each one touched off by some predicated tie to, or transformation of, the initial set of categories. There may be a big story and a variety of little stories, and these of course can change their status over time. What we wish to bring out here is how the category-generated stories that make the Montreal Massacre an observable, news-reportable, members' phenomenon are made formally possible by the simple norm-based relationship expressed in the phrase "character appears on cue." The stories themselves—of crime, horror, tragedy, gun control, the killer, what we call in contradistinction to the last the "killer's story," and the story of violence against women—these we take up in the succeeding chapters.

CHAPTER 3

The Stories of Crime, Horror, Tragedy, Gun Control, and the Killer

INTRODUCTION

IN THE LAST CHAPTER WE CONSIDERED the various story characters who appeared on cue in relation to different aspects of the phenomenon of the Montreal Massacre. For the telling of different stories, each of which offered a different conceptualization, as it were, the arrival on the scene of a restricted collection of categorial incumbents was both unsurprising and appropriate, both reasonable and unremarkable. That it was so arose from the stories' reliance and dependence on taken for granted category-organizational resources. In this chapter we now turn to several of the particular stories themselves and examine in more detail their organizational accomplishment.

THE CRIME STORY

As noted in chapter 2, what the reader gets initially is a *crime* story founded in the standardized relational pair of categories "offender" and "victim(s)," and in the membership categorization device we called "parties to a homicide investigation" (PHI). The reported event is a mass killing that quickly becomes a "mass murder." The "offender" becomes a "killer." For about a week it's a detective story, as follows:

E32   MAN IN MONTREAL KILLS 14 WITH RIFLE

A gunman went on a rampage at the University of Montreal last night, killing 14 people before shooting himself dead.

Police took away a second suspect in handcuffs an hour after the shootings began. Late last night, a heavily armed police tactical team was combing the six-storey engineering building of the Ecole Polytechnique, which is affiliated with the university, for a possible third suspect.

Claude St. Laurent, a spokesman for the Montreal police, said the man taken away in handcuffs was being questioned. Some students said they recognized the man as a part-time physics teacher, but police would not confirm that or release his name.

Police also would not release the name of the gunman or any of the 14 other dead people. (Dec 7 [1])

E33   Killer's letter blames feminists
Suicide note contains apparent hit list of 15 women

The man who killed 14 women and wounded 12 other people at the University of Montreal on Wednesday wrote a three-page suicide letter that began by saying he was going to die on Dec. 6.

The man, whom police identified last night as Marc Lepine, unleashed a vicious diatribe against women as the reason for the shooting rampage. Police revealed that the letter contained what appeared to be a hit list of 15 women, all Quebec personalities, apparently including one provincial cabinet minister.

Detectives refused to release the names, noting that each woman would be interviewed by police in the coming days.

Minutes before an afternoon news conference was to begin, homicide detectives learned the killer's identity. But Andre Tessier, head of the Montreal Urban Community criminal investigation division, refused to release the name. He said his detectives still had to get in touch with the man's family so that a member could make a positive identification. Police confirmed the killer's name later.

At the news conference, Jacques Duchesneau, director of MUC's organized crime unit, would not release the handwritten letter, which was found in Mr. Lepine's pocket. He said the letter was being analyzed forensically.

However, Mr. Duchesneau did highlight several points made by Mr. Lepine.

"First, he mentioned he was doing this for political reasons. He said feminists have always ruined his life; that he wasn't too happy in life, particularly in the last seven years; that he was rejected from the Canadian Army because he was not sociable; and he made a reference to Corporal Denis Lortie, saying he was only doing what Mr. Lortie did."

(Mr. Lortie killed three people with a machine-gun in the Quebec National Assembly on May 8, 1984.)

Mr. Duchesneau said a photograph of Mr. Lepine had been taken at the morgue for distribution to the news media, but it was not released because police had discovered the man's identity "just a minute before we came into the room."

Mr. Tessier said police got the name through the store where Mr. Lepine purchased the semi-automatic rifle he used on his killing rampage. He added that Mr. Lepine legally bought the Mini-14 semi-automatic rifle made by Sturm, Ruger and Co. of Southport, Conn.

Mr. Lepine apparently had filled out the required forms with Quebec provincial police and was issued a gun permit after a check was done to determine whether he had a criminal record.

"We know he bought the gun...[sic] that he was issued a certificate for the gun...[sic] and from that we know what his name is, but we have to make a certain number of checks before we could release that information," Mr. Tessier said.

Mr. Duchesneau described the rifle as "the same type used by the U.S. armed forces...[sic] It's the type of weapon you could buy for hunting reasons."

Mr. Duchesneau said police still have not determined why Mr. Lepine chose the University of Montreal to carry out his vendetta against women.

Louis Courville, interim director of the polytechnical institute where the shooting occurred, said he had the feeling that the killer had visited the school before because he seemed to be quite familiar with the layout.

Mr. Courville added that a check of school records showed that Mr. Lepine was not a student and had "no connection to the school." Witnesses said they could not recall ever seeing Mr. Lepine in the school at any time before Wednesday.

Police said a check of Mr. Lepine's fingerprints with the RCMP in Ottawa revealed no leads, indicating that he had no criminal record.

In a reconstruction of the killing rampage, Mr. Duchesneau said that shortly after 5:15 p.m. on Wednesday, Mr. Lepine, dressed in a hunting outfit and wearing a baseball hat emblazoned with Montreal Tracteur (Montreal Tractor), entered the Ecole Polytechnique and went to the second floor.

Mr. Duchesneau said Mr. Lepine shot his first victim in a hallway and burst into a classroom where he ordered the men and women to stand at separate ends of the room. Many of the students thought it was a joke, but they stopped laughing when he fired a shot into the ceiling.

Mr. Lepine then told the men to leave and killed six women. He calmly walked out of the classroom and headed for the first-floor cafeteria, where he killed three more women. Then he went to the third floor, where he killed four more women in another classroom before turning the rifle on himself.

At the news conference, Chief Coroner Jean Grenier said all the victims have been identified and the families have been advised. Then, to a hushed room, he read the names of the 14 dead women. He said autopsies were being carried out. (Dec 8 [1])

E34   Police suspected more than 1 sniper was loose in school

Conflicting reports by eyewitnesses Wednesday night had led police to believe that more than one sniper was loose inside the Ecole Polytechnique and responsible for the rampage that left 15 people dead, including the gunman, and 12 wounded.

...

At 6:30 p.m., two hours after the killings, police arrested one suspect inside the building. He was taken to be questioned and later released. An hour later, heavily armed tactical squad members were seen entering the building, presumably in search of other suspects. (Dec 8 [9])

E35   Jacques Duchesneau, director of the organized crime division of the Montreal Urban Community police, said Mr. Lepine legally purchased the rifle on Nov. 21 in the Montreal area. Mr. Lepine had been issued a gun permit after a check was done to determine that he had no criminal record.

Throughout the day, homicide detectives and journalists worked feverishly, trying to piece together more personal information on the man who systematically and calmly slaughtered 14 young women. (Dec 9 [3])

E36   So far, police have been unable to link Mr. Lepine to any of his 14 young victims... One of the 14 women massacred last week at the University of Montreal was stabbed to death, not shot like the other victims, police say.

...

"Lepine still had some bullets left," Mr. Tessier noted. "Why did he use a knife in this case? We don't know. It seems he was crazy with rage, determined to kill any way he could."

Police first said all 14 women had been shot, but ensuing autopsies revealed Ms Leclair's stabbing.

The knife had no trace of blood on it when it was found, having been wiped clean by the killer, police say. (Dec 11 [1])

E37   More massacre details to be released by police, but an inquiry ruled out. (Dec 12 [3])

E38   **Police refusal to answer questions leaves lots of loose ends in killings**

Investigators have appealed to witnesses of the shooting rampage to come forward with any information.

Meanwhile, police have found a rental car near the University of Montreal that was apparently rented by Mr. Lepine on the day of the killings. (Dec 13 [1])

The standardized relational pair "offender (killer)/victims" occasions the relevance of PHI and therefore of the appearance of police and police-predicated activities. The crime story is then made up of reports of police tasks—identifying the dead killer and the victims, informing victims' next-of-kin, determining if there were accomplices (arresting and searching for further suspects), interviewing others involved, handling physical evidence, checking out the weapon, giving or refusing to give statements to the media, locating a motive (for example, seeking a relationship between the killer and (any of the) victims, and analyzing the relevance of the suicide letter), determining who the killer was as a course-of-action type (did he have a criminal record?), and determining the killer's course of action at the scene. But as big crime stories go, this one is short-lived, since its projected career through the criminal justice system—each stage providing an opportunity for further activities and for their reporting—is foreclosed by the killer having killed himself. There will be no search for the killer and no arrest, charging, bail hearing, preliminary hearing, jury selection, trial, or sentencing. Moreover, the killer has announced his motive and left a letter identifying himself and explaining his actions.

Although truncated, the crime story nevertheless frames the early reporting as the reporters follow the categories to the police station and the police news conferences. The very obviousness of this step conceals the evaluation of the event that the step entails. What the killer wanted to be seen as a political act, presumably transcending or suspending its possible status as a crime, is treated in the reporting *as* crime (cf. Hester and Eglin 1992: chap. 6) and, as a particular kind of crime, namely mass murder, it is furnished with context and taken up in commentary:

E39   Systematic slaughter is without precedent. MICHAEL VALPY. (Dec 8 [6])

E40   Mass murders not increasing, Canadian anthropologist says. (Dec 8 [10])

E41   *Canada's past includes other mass shootings* [list provided]. (Dec 8 [11])

To characterize the Montreal murders as a "mass murder," making them an instance of the collection "mass murders" and comparing them with other instances in the collection, is to take a particular interpretative step. We consider the significance of that step in chapter 4 when reviewing the killer's course of action from his point of view.

THE HORROR STORY

The first day's coverage in the *Globe and Mail* consists of two articles. Much of the first article (reproduced in chapter 2), and the whole of the second (reproduced below), is devoted to witnesses' descriptions of what happened. Many of these vignettes tell what is recognizably a *horror story* (see Johnson 1995) founded in a "terrifying scene," marked by people "screaming," "shouting," and "yelling" (Dec 7 [2]), and from which "scores of horrified students streamed" (Dec 7 [1]). Here is the whole of the second article:

E42   Terrified students describe shooting scene
Canadian Press
Montreal

Here's how witnesses recall the terrifying scene as a gunman began firing at random in a packed classroom at the University of Montreal yesterday:

"I was doing a presentation in front of the class and suddenly a guy came in with what I think was a semi-automatic rifle," said Eric Chavarie, an engineering student.

"He told us to stop everything.

"And then, when we looked at him, we thought it was a joke, but he fired a shot in the air and separated us into two groups, the guys in one corner and the girls in (another) corner.

"When that was done, he asked the guys to leave. He left the girls in there.

"We got outside in the hallway and for a couple of minutes he stayed in there and after, when we got out, he levelled his gun at a group of people who were there and he shot three or four shots."

Pierre Robert, 25, a student in the classroom, said: "He told the guys to move to one side and the girls to the other. Nobody moved. We thought it was joke. It was our last hour of the term. We practically laughed.

"I thought it was a blank," said Mr. Robert, who was close to the classroom wall at which the gunman fired. "I didn't see anything on the wall. But it made a very loud noise.

"When he came in he was really calm, but after the first shot his voice became nervous."

Yvon Bouchard, who taught the mechanical engineering course and was sitting at his desk listening to the student presentation when the gunman entered, said: "I didn't see him walk in. When I saw him, he was two or three feet from the students presenting their project.

"Then he asked all the men to go to one side of the room and the women on the other. Nobody moved. We thought it was a joke.

"It doesn't make sense."

Luc Gauthier, 24, a student who left the classroom about 5 p.m. when the gunman entered carrying an object that looked like a rifle in a trash bag, said: "I went to the bathroom and when I came back people were running out, screaming, 'There's a crazy guy in there. He's shot people.'"

"I went to get my things and saw there was blood in front of the photocopy machine. Someone told me the first person he shot when he came out of the classroom was a girl in front of the photo-copy machine."

Francois Bordeleau, a student who ran from the first to the second floor and dragged people by the collar to keep them from going downstairs to see the gunman, said: "It was a human hunt. We were the quarry.

"I heard the gunman say, 'I want the women,'" he said. "I was too far away to see his face, but if he'd seen me I was finished."

Mr. Bordeleau said the gunman "would fire, then advance, pull down on his gun (as if to reload or cock it), fire another shot, then move forward and shoot."

Student Serge Bacon said: "I was in the stairwell and some-one came up the stairs shouting, 'Watch out! Watch out! He's com-ing!' I thought he was joking."

Yannick Lacoste, a student who had just left the school library when she heard about five consecutive gunshots in the hallways, said: "People were yelling, 'Someone is firing,' and students were running through the halls.

"I hurried to the door. I was very nervous. You don't know if the shots are aimed at you." (Dec 7 [2])

The killing of fourteen members of the "enemy" during wartime may be described as a "routine ambush" or "skirmish" or, indeed, a "massacre" if the circumstances warrant (as in My Lai). On a university or college campus where the institutionalized identities are "student," "teacher," "member of staff," and so on (Sharrock and Button 1991: 159), the transformation of category identi-ties to "offender," "victim," "witness," and so on invoked by the killing of four-teen "students" occasions florid reportage in terms of a horrific scene. In the

Globe and Mail, the event is referred to as follows: a "rampage" (Dec 7 [1]; Dec 8 [9]; Dec 11 [1]) "shooting rampage" (Dec 8 [1]; Dec 9 [3]; Dec 12 [3]), "killing rampage" (Dec 8 [1]), "massacre" (Dec 8 [2], [7], [9]; Dec 9 [1], [2], [6]; Dec 11 [1], [4]; Dec 12 [1], [2], [3], [4], [5]; Dec 13 [1]; Dec 16 [1]), "The Massacre in Montreal" (Dec 8 [4]; Dec 12 [2]), "the Montreal massacre" (Dec 8 [3], [10]; Dec 16 [1]), "massacre at the University of Montreal" (Dec 13 [2]), "slaughter" (Dec 12 [2], [3]), "wanton slaughter" (Dec 8 [4]), "systematic slaughter" (Dec 8 [6]), "mass slaughter" (Dec 9 [6]), "mass murder(s)" (Dec 8 [6], [8], [10]; Dec 11 [1], [3], [4]; Dec 12 [1]), "mass shootings" (Dec 8 [11]), "horrifying executions" (Dec 8 [3]), "slaying" (Dec 13 [1], [3]), "brutal slaying" (Dec 11 [1]), "bloodbath" (Dec 8 [9]), "carnage" (Dec 9 [1]), the "violence in Montreal" (Dec 9 [5], [6]), the "University of Montreal murders" (Dec 12 [6]), "the bloodiest crime in Quebec's modern history" (Dec 16 [1]).

The horror, we want to say, turns on the disjuncture between the membership categories made relevant by the setting and those made relevant by the event *when a character appears who is definitely NOT on cue*. That he is not on cue is not at first appreciated by parties to the scene. They evidently attempt to normalize his appearance by invoking an available feature of the context, namely that this was the last class of the term in this course and someone was exploiting the occasion to stage a prank or joke. It is relevant to note the formal similarity, if not identity, in the structure of horror and comedy here. Both turn on the incongruity between setting and action.[1]

Thus, in the first day's coverage many of the reported reactions of witnesses turn on the disjuncture between setting-related and event-based categories and their conventional predicates, as follows:

E43   "I was doing a presentation in front of the class and suddenly a guy came in with what I think was a semi-automatic rifle.... And then, when we looked at him, we thought it was joke." (Dec 7 [2])

E44   "We thought it was a joke, then the man fired a shot, and all hell broke loose." (Dec 7 [1])

E45   "I saw death close up and I shook," said Vanthona Ouy, 22, one of scores of horrified students who streamed out of the building. (Dec 7 [1])

E46   "It was a human hunt," he said. "We were the quarry." (Dec 7 [1]; Dec 7 [2]).

E47   "I went to the bathroom and when I came back people were running out, screaming, 'There's a crazy guy in there. He's shot people.'"

"I went to get my things and saw there was blood in front of the photocopy machine. Someone told me the first person he shot when he came out of the classroom was a girl in front of the photocopy machine." (Dec 7 [2])

E48   [As we noted in chapter 2, Pierre Leclair, director of public relations
for the Montreal Police,] arrived at the scene of the bloodbath to find
his daughter lying dead on the floor…in a pool of blood. (Dec 8
[9])

What is horrific, then, is: someone carrying a gun, and shooting a gun, not
at a target range, but in a classroom during a class (E43–E44); taking part in a
class, then seeing a classmate killed before your eyes (E45); being a human
being but feeling like a hunted animal (E46); going to the bathroom, then being
told someone is shooting people, then passing the photocopying machine and
seeing blood in front of it (E47); going to a place to do your job, but finding
your daughter there dead in a pool of blood (E48) (see Hester 1992). What is horrific is the desecration involved when the routine, "settinged" activities and
objects of a college campus are turned into the scene of bloody murder. The
reporting, that is, expresses revulsion at this breach of the bodily and social
integrity of everyday life incarnate in the categorial organization made available in the institutionalized setting of a mundane place.

▼
THE TRAGEDY

A third story comprising the Montreal Massacre is that of *tragedy,* a term used
routinely throughout the coverage to describe the event, notably on the occasion of vigils, funerals and memorial services. For example, in "Thousands of
mourners wait in silence to pay final respects to slain women" it is reported that:

E49   Hundreds of telegrams—from schools, student associations, government officials and women's groups—lined the walls leading to
the hall. People read them intently, as if they might hold some explanation for the *tragedy.* (Dec 11 [1] emphasis added)

While the otherwise odd collection of sources of the telegrams is partially
accountable in terms of the setting and categorizations of the victims, the presence of "government officials" in the list makes available what is otherwise
not a separable story line, namely that the massacre is a public disaster. Just
how what we nevertheless want to call the "public disaster" *story* is accountable in the coverage is an interesting question, which we take up in chapter 7.

What is evident from the reportage is that the story of personal tragedy at
least is seen to reside in the victims' loss of their future lives, and the consequent
losses entailed for their relatives and friends. The tragedy, that is, is formally
located in the organization of two membership categorization devices, namely
the stage-of-life device (Sacks 1974; Atkinson 1980) and "R," the collection of
standardized relational pairs introduced in chapter 1. In terms of the stage-
of-life device the victims are describable as "young people," and, as such, may
expect the conventional future predicated of the category "young person."

Moreover, that anticipated future is shaped by the expectations of "success" conventionally associated with the particular category of young person called "student." The tragedy is founded in the affront to the value expressed in the right to life and security of the person, and in the social expectation of a successful life to come, when *students* get death instead of degrees.

E50   "The tragedy which unfolded at l'Ecole Polytechnique compels us to live the absurd and the suffering with an ever greater intensity," Cardinal Gregoire continued. "Fourteen young women were brutally mowed down in the beauty of their youth when everything seemed to assure them of a brilliant future, useful to society.

"In a few moments, a desperate and aberrant act of another young person was enough to destroy all the dreams, all the promises["]. (Dec 12 [1])

The tragedy is located in the disjuncture between the predicated and actual futures of these murdered young people, these dead students.

The tragedy is further based in the interruption of family and collective biographies.

E51   They came to mourn and they came to say a final, tearful goodbye to their daughters, their sisters, their friends. (Dec 12 [1])

The terms of description here—daughters, sisters, friends—are made relevant by the categorial organization of R, in which they are tied to their respective pair parts, parents, brothers/sisters, friends. The deaths become events in the lives of those referred to in terms of the categories naming their respective pair parts (Drew 1978: 15). Such deaths become tragic when they are unexpected, since, in part, R organizes relationships specifically for the purpose of engaging in "the search for help" (Sacks 1967, 1972). When death comes suddenly in the family, when your best friend is killed, incumbents of the related pair parts are denied the opportunity to provide the very sort of life-saving help their category position makes them available, and obligates them, to give. The disjuncture is particularly acute in the case of the police officer who is, as it were, especially obligated to come to the assistance of those in trouble, but arrives at a scene at which there is nothing he can do to bring help to his own dead daughter. The category-predicate disjunctures are what make the tragedy, as the tragedy makes the news, and does so recognizably (Anderson and Sharrock 1979: 380–81; Hester and Eglin 1997c: 42, 45; Johnson 1995: 22–23).

When the newspaper quotes interviews with family members, both forms of tragic loss are made available together. For example:

E52   Parents of some of the young women who died in the massacre expressed shock and horror. Clarence Colgan talked about his daughter Helene as if she was still alive.

"Helene is so enthusiastic, so lovely, so vivacious, so full of life," the 50-year-old father said yesterday in a halting, sombre voice.

Then he stopped.

"I guess that should be was, you know, past tense. Helene is dead, isn't she. She's not, she's not here."

...

"She wanted to go to the farthest limits of life," her father said. "She had so much ambition and hope and, oh Lord, I don't even want to think what she could have done."

Claude Daigneault was the one who had to call his brothers and sisters to let them know their niece, Barbara, was dead at the age of 22.

"My brother, Barbara's father, was certain she wasn't involved in the shootings," said Mr. Daigneault.

"He heard about it on the radio, but he kept telling himself that it couldn't happen to Barbara—even though she hadn't telephoned to say she was all right.["] (Dec 8 [9])

E53 **Helene Colgan,** 23, was in her final year of mechanical engineering and planned to take her master's degree. "She was as good a student as they come," said her father, Clarence. "She worked enormously hard and read everything that came to hand. She wanted to go to the farthest limits of life. She had so much ambition and hope...I don't even want to think what she could have done." She had three job offers and was leaning toward accepting one from a company based near Toronto. Her best friend, Nathalie Croteau, was also killed.

Nathalie Croteau, 23, another graduating mechanical engineer, planned to leave Dec. 29 for a two-week vacation in Cancun, Mexico, with Ms Colgan. Her father, Fernand Croteau, is a laboratory technician in suburban Brossard. "Twenty-three years aimed at graduating with a degree," he said. "Her life has been taken away from her just when it was starting to look as if all that effort would be paying off. It doesn't make sense." (Dec 11 [5])

Insofar, then, as the categorial organization of the stage-of-life device and R guide the selection of events to which reporters are assigned, and the selection of interviews and other speech they report, then we may find that embedded in the reporting of the event is a further commentary on it. Losses are to be mourned, tragedies lamented. Thus the newspaper gives brief obituaries, in most cases based on interviews with family members in which the victim is described in terms of character and anticipated future (Dec 11 [5]), family members' heartfelt reactions are quoted (Dec 8 [9]), and reporters follow the categories to the funerals to quote the eulogies that reflexively warrant their stories (Dec 11 [1]; Dec 12 [1]; Dec 13 [2]).

▼
THE GUN CONTROL STORY

What we get, further, is a *political story about gun control.* The killer is a "gun-man" from the start, who killed "with a rifle." Moreover, to repeat extract 35 from above:

E35   Jacques Duchesneau, director of the organized crime division of the Montreal Urban Community police, said Mr. Lepine legally purchased the rifle on Nov. 21 in the Montreal area. Mr. Lepine had been issued a gun permit after a check was done to determine that he had no criminal record. (Dec 9 [3])

But since "gun control" is a public policy issue, this is a theme with political ramifications. It provides one sense in which the story is political. Reporters are assigned, the issue reviewed, and interviews held with relevant politicians (Dec 8 [8]; Dec 9 [4]; Dec 11 [6]; *KWR,* Dec 7 [5]; *KWR,* Dec 12 [3]). Again, the structure and content of the reporting implies an evaluation and commentary on the significance of the event. This is a matter of political responsibility. Indeed, part of the *tragedy,* implies the story, is that the deaths may have been preventable had the proposed legislation been passed that would have banned the type of weapon used in the killings. Gun control is a story that is touched off by an aspect of the offender's demeanour in the *crime* story: he killed with a gun. As we shall see in subsequent chapters, it can be found in conjunction with the "mass murder" and "violence-in-society" interpretations of the killings. This is a story that has persisted to the present, and deserves a fuller recounting than we are prepared to give here. Our reasons for giving it short shrift are simply that, first, it quickly moves away from the substance of the massacre, and second, and partly for that reason, we can find little of interest in relation to membership categorization analysis to say about the topic.[2]

▼
THE STORY ABOUT THE KILLER

What we get also, and inevitably, is a story about a *killer,* the offender himself (Dec 8 [1]; Dec 9 [3]; Dec 11 [1], [3]; Dec 12 [3]; Dec 13 [1]). As we noted in chapter 2 (see extract E3), the conceptual grammar that embraces criminal act, motive, and biography-and-social-background guides the reporting to the predicated sources, the police, the coroner (for example, the question of the disposal of the body (Dec 12 [3]; Dec 13 [1]), the neighbours, the neighbourhood stores, the landlord, the family, the mother's divorce records, the friends, the school, the college, the army recruitment office. In chapter 2, that is, we were concerned to bring out how the initial categorizations constituting the event as a crime story, namely "offender/victims," provided for the relevance, via the device PHI, of reporting the words of other categories of persons now as "witnesses." Our interest there was in focusing on the *categories*. Here our interest is in the *story* the newspaper tells about the killer via those witnesses. It is a story built with the resources provided by the initial characterization of the events as a crime. That is, it is initially embedded in the crime story, then developed into a story of its own. Here is the full text of the principal article telling that story, followed by relevant extracts from the others.

E54 *Killer fraternized with men in army fatigues*

Marc Lepine, who killed 14 women and wounded 12 other people in a shooting rampage at the University of Montreal on Wednesday, hung out with a small band of men who walked around their neighborhood wearing army fatigues.

Employees at a grocery store across the street from the killer's flat on a narrow street just east of the downtown core said yesterday that Mr. Lepine and his friends rented war and violent action films from a nearby video store.

"They loved watching army and violent films," one employee said. "But they never caused any trouble around here. Sometimes they would go into (a local) gun shop and admire the weapons."

Another employee said Mr. Lepine, 25, would sometimes make caustic comments about women. "He did not like feminists... women taking (traditional) men's jobs. He often spoke out against career women and he blamed his problem with getting into university on women (being accepted in such areas as engineering)."

At a nearby camping and hunting supply store, a clerk said Mr. Lepine was a frequent visitor, going in from time to time to buy camouflage apparel and admire the rifles and handguns.

However, the clerk said he was certain that Mr. Lepine did not purchase the semi-automatic rifle he used in his killing rampage from his store.

The weapon, made by Sturm, Ruger and Co. of Southport, Conn., is described in the company's sales brochures as "ideal for law enforcement." Gun shop owners in Montreal said the high-powered, .223-calibre, paramilitary rifle, which sells for about $600, is popular with hunters.

Jacques Duchesneau, director of the organized crime division of the Montreal Urban Community police, said Mr. Lepine legally purchased the rifle on Nov. 21 in the Montreal area. Mr. Lepine had been issued a gun permit after a check was done to determine that he had no criminal record.

Throughout the day, homicide detectives and journalists worked feverishly, trying to piece together more personal information on the man who systematically and calmly slaughtered 14 young women.

Oddly, police could not turn up any evidence that Mr. Lepine had ever received any psychiatric treatment.

Mr. Lepine was born Gamil Gharbi on Oct. 26, 1964, in Montreal to a French-Canadian mother and an Algerian father. His parents split up when he was 7, leaving his sister and himself to live with their mother. His father lives abroad. His sister and mother, who identified her son's body, live in Montreal. In 1982, he changed his name legally to his mother's maiden name.

Mr. Lepine spent his first three years of secondary school at St. Thomas High School in Pointe Claire and the last two years at the Polyvalente des Sources in Pierrefonds. He then attended St. Laurent CEGEP (community college) for three years, stud[y]ing sciences. He took a fourth year to study electronics.

Claude Boilly, director of the CEGEP, said teachers vaguely remember Mr. Lepine.

Mr. Boilly said one department head "couldn't really put a face to him because he was a low-profile student although he got the fourth highest mark in his course and he (the teacher) told me he seems to remember that (Mr. Lepine) had talked about attending Ecole Polytechnique" at the University of Montreal.

Police said Mr. Lepine had also taken a computer course at Control Data Institute and "an update" night course in chemistry at the CEGEP Vieux Montreal with the aim of being accepted by the Ecole Polytechnique, the engineering school where he carried out his murderous assault.

Mr. Lepine, who was unemployed, was recently fired from a job at a Montreal-area hospital, police added.

In a three-page suicide letter, Mr. Lepine mentioned that he had tried to get into the Canadian army but was rejected because he was "anti-social."

Major Serge Quenneville, a spokesman for the Canadian Forces in Montreal, confirmed that Mr. Lepine had applied in the winter of 1980–81 under his former name and was rejected.

Major Quenneville refused to say why his application was rejected. The form has been turned over to police in Montreal.

He said it was up to Montreal police to release any details about Mr. Lepine's application. All he would say was that Mr. Lepine applied in person at the recruiting office in downtown Montreal when he was about 18.

Meanwhile, scores of journalists descended yesterday morning on the neighborhood where Mr. Lepine lived from the summer of 1987. Neighbours said he shared a $285-a-month, five-room, second-floor flat with a young, blond man named Eric.

They described Mr. Lepine as an ordinary man, somewhat of an introvert who was quiet and courteous, although he sometimes stayed up late playing loud music. None could believe that he was capable of mass murder.

Maurice Dutrisac, his landlord, said he was shocked to learn that Mr. Lepine had committed the murders. "He was a quiet person. Always polite. I am surprised he did this."

Mr. Dutrisac said he had visited the flat on occasion and had never noticed anything amiss, such as bizarre posters on the walls or weapons in any of the rooms.

He also said Mr. Lepine always mailed his rental cheque before the first of the month, but he had not received payment for December. (Dec 9 [3])

E55   Details about Mr. Lepine's life that continue to emerge show a man fascinated by computers and war-game videos who was apparently an abused child. His parents separated when he was seven years old and divorced eight years later.

At a 1976 divorce hearing, his mother, Monique Lepine, described her husband, Liass Gharbi, as a brutal father who had contempt for women and believed they were intended only to serve men.

"He was a very brutal man who did not have any control of his emotions," she testified, adding her husband beat Marc, sometimes leaving marks on his face that lasted a week and at other times bloodying his nose. At the time, Mr. Gharbi denied the allegations.

The marriage so scarred Monique Lepine, Marc and his sister Nadia that they spent a year in psychotherapy. "We had difficulties expressing love," the mother told her divorce hearing.

During his youth, Mr. Lepine spent some of his summers with uncles hunting, said a source close to the family who asked not to be named. Mr. Lepine probably learned to shoot from an uncle who had trained with the elite U.S. Special Forces, better known as the Green Berets, and had been a Canadian Forces paratrooper, the sources said. (Dec 11 [1])

E56   about Marc Lepine, the 25-year-old unemployed man...

Detectives also visited the second-storey flat, just east of the downtown Montreal core, where Mr. Lepine lived with a male friend.

In a peculiar twist, Mr. Lepine stabbed Maryse Leclair—his last victim—to death after apparently wounding her with rifle fire. He then turned the gun on himself.

The 23-year-old engineering student was the daughter of Pierre Leclair, director of communications for the MUC police force.

Mr. Leclair's cousin, Louis-Marie Leclair, is the director of a Laval hospital where Mr. Lepine once worked as a kitchen helper before being fired. (Dec 13 [1])

The story of the killer is told in terms of the following matters: what he did, that is, who he killed and how he killed them; where he acquired the murder weapon, and how he learned to shoot; his possible relationship to one of his victims; where he lived and who with, his domestic demeanour and rent-paying habit; who his friends were, how they all dressed, and what he and they did for entertainment; what he liked to buy and what he admired, in the way of leisure equipment; his summer pastime; what he could be heard to say about women; his age, place of birth, parentage, ethnic background, and change of name; his home life, his parents' separation and divorce, his father's personality and attitudes towards women, the domestic violence, the abuse he suffered, the family's therapeutic history, the absence of a psychiatric record for him; his secondary and tertiary education, the subjects he studied, what he was like as a student, his educational ambitions; his attempt to enter the military; his recent employment history and employment status. But though these are very much like the standard terms informing the questions on a social survey, the particular answers they afford are not the result of a disinterested sociological inquiry. Rather they are predicates comprising the grammar of the concept "killer." That is, since the act is taken to be deviant, its agent must be deviant too. Deviance not only demands explanation but explanation of a culturally adequate sort. The (unreported) reporter's questions and the sort of answers both given and deemed fit to report are accountable in the terms of such a cultural grammar. The grammar generates the terms of the inquiry and the sort of responses that are seen to *be* answers. The point has been made in the early ethnomethodological work of Blum and McHugh (1971) on the social ascription of motives, of Smith (1975) on mental illness and of Atkinson (1978) on suicide, and has been elaborated in considerable detail by Jayyusi (1984). We will not repeat such analysis again here. Rather we may point to the summary social-psychological profile that appears in the headlines and commentary as exhibiting the conventional terms of the grammar—that is, it comprises a biography of troubles and a disordered social background:

E57   **Marc Lepine: abused child who grew up to be a quitter.** (*KWR*, Dec 11 [2])

E58   **"He'd never ask for help"**
The murderer of 14 university women grew up with a brutal father. (*KWR*, Dec 12 [4])

E59   **Litany of social ills created Marc Lepine**
Marc Lepine fits to a T the mass murderer's profile. The loner, pathologically alienated from the supports of close friends and family.

The person imbued with the sense of powerlessness over his own life in a world of larger and larger impersonal institutions. The devotee of Rambo cultural imagery, seeing in it the solution to the individual's societal impotence.

...

It is the social conditions that produce Marc Lepine—and more and more Marc Lepines—that concern me. (Dec 11 [3])

Although it is revealed in the reporting that the killer had a plan, had bought a gun and rented a car, that his target was "feminists" (including a "hit list") and his motive was "political," nevertheless neither the *Globe and Mail* nor the *Kitchener-Waterloo Record* pursues the "political angle" in their reporting.[4] Though one tiny article in each paper reports that, respectively, a "Violent film on terrorists preceded tragedy" (Dec 9 [2]), and "TV aired movie of terror in the classroom" (*KWR*, Dec 9 [2]), and one commentator (Sasha McInnes) is reported asserting in an open letter to men "This is a men's issue, this is men's violence; this terrorism and these deaths are your creations and your shame" (Dec 11 [4]), the newspaper does not call the killer a terrorist, nor is he compared to other terrorists. His political goals are not elaborated, the question of the efficacy of his methods not raised. Rather, as we have already noted, he is framed by a list the newspaper provides of previous "mass murders" (Dec 8 [11]), quite a different scheme of interpretation. The structure and content of the reporting, based in the categories of description employed, exhibits a preference for viewing him as an instance of social pathology rather than as the "rational erudite" he sought to be. This, then, is a story about a killer, but not, except in briefest part, the "killer's story." This, too, then, is an embedded commentary informing the Montreal Massacre as a members' phenomenon.

It is also a view that stands in marked contrast to the idea, which we examine in the next chapter, that "he was not a very politically astute man, but he was, as terrorists are, more political than the people who try to understand him socially or psychologically." (McCormack 1990: 32)

CHAPTER 4

The Killer's Story

▼
INTRODUCTION: CRIME AS ACCOUNTABLE ACTION

Studies of criminal and deviant BEHAVIOUR rarely address seriously the naturally occurring accounts of the criminals and deviants themselves. Where they *have* been considered, as in the symbolic interactionist studies of Cressey (1953), Matza (1964) and Scott and Lyman (1970), they have been adduced from after-the-event interview materials and have then been re-presented as decontextualized and generalized and quasi-causal explanations of deviant behaviour.[1] Furthermore, as we observe below, members of society, including criminals and deviants, do not as a rule formulate explicitly the grounds of their actions in the course of doing them. As such, the analytic potential of our present materials is rich. They afford not only an opportunity to explore issues of interest to membership categorization analysis, they can also be used in the discovery and investigation of the "lost causes," as it were, of criminal and deviant behaviour as *accountable action.*

One of the most unfortunate legacies of the various structuralist critiques that bullied their way onto the sociological scene in the 1960s and 1970s was the conventional wisdom that interpretive approaches such as symbolic interactionism and ethnomethodology had nothing to say about the causes of human action. Such a misconception was founded in a very narrow view of such a topic, namely that causes can only be investigated in terms of a positivist model of the relation between antecedent determinative factors and ensuing outcomes. Symbolic interactionism in this regard was held to have paid scant regard to the causes of "primary deviation" and to have been excessively preoccupied with the causes [*sic*] of secondary deviation. Our view is that this is a profoundly mistaken view of symbolic interactionism as the work of Becker, Matza, and others attests, where, we note, there is a concentration on causality at the level of meaning. Arguably, the symbolic interactionists, not unlike Weber, fused interpretivism with positivism, a confusion that perhaps goes some way to explaining the lack of success, beyond the production of ethnographic studies, of this particular sociological genre (see Hester and Eglin 1992: 12–13, 111–113).

If symbolic interactionism was found wanting at the font of causality, ethnomethodology was never considered even to be a marginal member of the congregation. Rightly so, of course, since it was indifferent to positivism from the beginning. However, this does not mean that ethnomethodology cannot address issues such as the causes of crime. Indeed, it is our view that the seminal work of Sacks on the "Search for Help" provides a way to address interpretively and adequately this very question. Far from being a "lost cause," then, ethnomethodology, we argue, can illuminate those "causes" that are lost at the very inception of positivist and structuralist studies. Thus, action in ethnomethodology is regarded as accountable, as the product of human reasoning and analysis. The conclusion, in Sacks's famous study, that suicidal persons "have no one to turn to" is shown to have been reached through a "category search."

The Sacksian model can be applied to any action. Of course, not all actions may involve a category search and, indeed, for many actions, categorial considerations may not be relevant. But many actions are carried out under the auspices of such considerations; the reasoning that precedes them can be shown to have involved categorial dimensions of various kinds. In this connection, we note that one of the most appreciative of symbolic interactionist studies, that of Athens (1980), can be recast in categorial terms. Athens's concern was primarily to demonstrate that violence is not some "mindless" event but that, even in the heat of the moment, there is an "inner dialogue," a consciousness of self and other, a working out of action from interpretation and judgement. However, his data from interviews with convicted murderers, rapists, and the like, can be used to show that membership categories were pivotal in the courses of human action that resulted in others' demise, injury, molestation, degradation, and the rest.

A similar conclusion is warranted on the basis of Watson's (1990, 1983; see also Wowk 1984) work on murderers' accounts of their actions in police interrogations. Thus, he indicates that, again, membership categories were key features of the reasoning that apparently led to the offences.

There are, of course, problems involved in drawing conclusions from retrospective accounts and then applying them *ex post facto* as antecedents. Indeed, we would not wish to give the impression that Watson intended his analyses to be treated in this way. However, along with Sacks, they do at least suggest the fruitfulness of examining the possibility that categorial ordering work may be involved in the course of human action. As it happens, and as we shall show in detail below, our data permit precisely such an examination, since the killer of the women in the Montreal Massacre made it perfectly plain that such a categorial ordering was central to his project.

▼
SACKS'S PROBLEM AND OUR PROBLEM

In "An Initial Investigation of the Usability of Conversational Data for Doing Sociology," Sacks (1972) poses his problem as "to construct a description that provides the reproduceability of the conclusion a suicidal person may reach— I have no one to turn to" (31). Finding a solution to this problem would mean, he writes, "attempting (a) to locate the collections of membership categories in terms of which the search for help for suicidalness is formulated, and (b) to describe the ways such collections are used to determine whether there are eligible persons available (to give "help")" (31–32). The collections of categories Sacks locates are what he called R, the collection of standardized relational pairs (husband-wife, parent-child, etc.), and K, the collection comprising the category classes "professionals" and "laypersons." As we mentioned in chapter 1, and have detailed elsewhere, in that study and in related work (Sacks 1974), he specified certain rules of use for categories from collections, such as the "economy rule," "consistency rule" and so on. A collection and its rules of use would then constitute a "membership categorization device." With such devices, he argued, members engaged in a search for help could find that they had "no one to turn to." Such a finding could be used as a rational basis for, say, attempting suicide (Sacks 1972: 49)

Sacks's model offers a method for investigating the accountability of action. In keeping with this model, we pose the following problem: How may we provide for the reproduceability, that is, the intelligibility or common-sense rationality (Eglin 1979a), of the two joined "conclusions" Marc Lépine apparently reached, that murder-followed-by-suicide was the solution to what he called his "political" problem? In particular, what part in his reasoning is *accountably* played by the local organization of the membership categories deployed in it? By "accountably" we mean "observably-reportably" (Garfinkel 1967), that is, "done in such a way that others can identify and report on what is being done."

▼
"YOU'RE ALL A BUNCH OF FEMINISTS": CATEGORIZATION AND THE POLITICS OF TERROR

As we have seen, the press reported at the time that on December 6, 1989, Lépine entered the Ecole polytechnique in Montreal and in its rooms and corridors shot dead thirteen female engineering students and a data processing worker, at the same time wounding another twelve persons there. The newspaper stories report witnesses' reports of what Lépine was heard saying at the scene.

E60   "I heard the gunman say: 'I want the women,'" Mr. Bordeleau said.
       That was confirmed by several other witnesses. (Dec 7 [1]; also
       [2])

E61   Ms Colgan, 23, was one of the 14 women shot to death Wednesday night when a young man wearing hunting clothes and yelling
"You're all feminists, I hate feminists" sprayed the halls and rooms
of the University of Montreal's engineering school with semi-automatic gunfire. (Dec 8 [9]; also [5], [3])

E62   Ms Provost said that when Mr. Lepine burst into her classroom,
ordering the male students to leave and the women to remain, she
tried to talk to him.
    "When we were alone with him in the room … [sic] he said, "I am
here to fight against feminism, that is why I am here." (Dec 9 [1])

E63   One student said the gunman threatened his cornered victims,
shouting: "You're women. You're going to be engineers. You're all a
bunch of feminists. I hate feminists!" (*KWR*, Dec 7 [1])

At the end of his "rampage" he is reported, according to police, to have shot himself dead.

Furthermore, it was reported that at a police news conference held on
December 7, a selective paraphrase was provided by the police of a "three-
page suicide letter" that had been found on him:

E64   However, Mr. Duchesneau did highlight several points made by
Mr. Lepine.
    "First, he mentioned he was doing this for political reasons. He
said feminists have always ruined his life; that he wasn't too happy
in life, particularly in the last seven years; that he was rejected from
the Canadian army because he was not sociable; and he made a
reference to Corporal Denis Lortie, saying he was only doing what
Mr. Lortie did." (Dec 8 [1])

Appended to the letter was what was called a "hit list" of prominent Quebec
feminists, the same article said.

The primary materials for the analysis offered here are the fullest version
of the killer's reported speech and the suicide letter. Here is that speech, laid
out schematically, as it was in a highlighted box on the front page of the *Kitchener-Waterloo Record* on December 7:

E65   **You're women.**
    You're going to be engineers.
    You're all a bunch of feminists.
    I hate feminists.

The editors of *The Montreal Massacre* (1991), Louise Malette and Marie Chalouh,
include in the English edition of the book the "Text of Marc Lepine's Suicide
Letter," preceded by an Editors' Note, as follows:

E66 *Soon after the Polytechnique massacre, reporter Francine Pelletier, whose name appeared on Marc Lepine's hit list, called upon author- ities to publish the complete letter the murderer carried with him when he committed suicide. The call went unanswered. However, a few weeks before the first anniversary of the massacre, Pelletier received a copy of the letter in the mail. With the consent of the editor,* **La Presse** *published the letter in its entirety in its Novem- ber 24, 1990 edition. Although its contents come as no surprise to us and do not really add to our knowledge of what happened, we nonetheless felt it would be useful to include the letter in the Eng- lish edition, if only because it was censored for almost a year and caused such controversy when it was finally published.*

> *This letter is reprinted with the kind permission of The Canadian Press News Limited.*

Forgive the mistakes, I had 15 minutes to write this.

See also Annex.

Would you also note that if I commit suicide today 89-12-06 it is not for economic reasons (for I have waited until I exhausted all my financial means, even refusing jobs) but for political reasons. Because I have decided to send the feminists, who have always ruined my life, to their Maker. For seven years life has brought me no joy and being totally blasé, I have decided to put an end to those viragos.

I tried in my youth to enter the Forces as a student-officer, which would have allowed me possibly to get into the arsenal and precede Lortie in a raid. They refused me because anti-social [*sic*]. I therefore had to wait until this day to execute my plans. In between, I continued my studies in a haphaz- ard way for they never really interested me, knowing in advance my fate. Which did not prevent me from obtaining very good marks despite my the- ory of not handing in work and the lack of studying before exams.

Even if the Mad Killer epithet will be attributed to me by the media, I consider myself a rational erudite that only the arrival of the Grim Reaper has forced to take extreme acts. For why persevere to exist if it is only to please the government. Being rather backward-looking by nature (except for science), the feminists have always enraged me. They want to keep the advantages of women (e.g. cheaper insurance, extended maternity leave preceded by a preventive leave etc.) while seizing for themselves those of men.

Thus it is an obvious truth that if the Olympic Games removed the Men-Women distinction, there would be Women only in the graceful events. So the feminists are not fighting to remove that barrier. They are so oppor- tunistic they neglect to profit from the knowledge accumulated by men through the ages. They always try to misrepresent them every time they can. Thus, the other day, I heard they were honoring the Canadian men and women who fought at the frontline during the world wars. How can you explain then that women were not authorized to go to the frontline??? Will we hear of Caesar's female legions and female galley slaves who of course took up 50 per cent of the ranks of history, though they never existed. [*sic*] A real Casus Belli.

Sorry for this too brief letter.

Marc Lépine.

The letter is followed by the 19-name list, with a note at the bottom:

Nearly died today. The lack of time (because I started too late) has allowed these radical feminists to survive.

Alea Jacta Est.

▼
LÉPINE'S PROBLEM

With respect to these materials, which we will consider in turn, we want to analyze the socio-logic of Lépine's "political" problem or, more accurately, his *two* problems: the accountability of the killings and his suicide. In so doing, we face, arguably, the same methodological question as Lépine himself, that is, to provide for the availability or visibility or observability-reportability, in short "accountability" (Garfinkel 1967), of his actions—first the murders and second his suicide—*as* political in the first place. Unlike the case of Lortie (referred to by Lépine in the letter and discussed below), Lépine's actions are not located, after all, in a setting where politics are institutionalized and so readily available as a *"socially sanctioned way* […] *of describing events in that setting"* (Sharrock and Button 1991: 159; see Hester and Eglin 1997d: 159–160). Lépine therefore faces the problem of making his victims available as "political" targets. In particular he faces the problem of making his targets visible *as* feminists, given that such an identification, or "category incumbency," is not conventionally available in the form of bodily or other insignia (Jayyusi 1984: 68–73):

> As compared with gender and stage-of-life category incumbencies, other categorial incumbencies are not so available on sight. Political beliefs, religious affiliations, etc. may be displayable in talk and action or through other interactionally available matters such as known-in-common persons' names, but are not naively taken to be available for the looking. They are essentially revelatory matters—objects for revelation—through first-person avowal, third-person report, discovery or close inspection of a variety of "objects" (talk, action, names, biography, residential location, records, profession, etc.).[3]

Since motives for suicide are not necessarily self-evident either, their rationality as political must also be made available somehow; it is for this reason that the suicide letter becomes part of the suicide's recipient design.

The announcement/denunciation

We want to characterize the killer's reported speech as a denunciation that contains also an announcement. That is, in denouncing feminists, he at the same time announces what he is doing. We begin with the announcing. Why might a person announce what it is they are doing in the course of doing it? After all, it is a commonplace of conversation analysis (CA) to point out that a characteristic of such spoken interaction is that interlocutors do *not* standardly formulate what actions their utterances are performing as a running accompaniment to those utterances. Rather they rely on the resource provided by "next turn" for other speakers to do an understanding check if required. Formulating the gist of the conversation *is* done by parties to the talk at particular points for particular purposes (Heritage and Watson 1979), but not because there is some general deficiency carried by all talk's utterances that requires they be supplemented by a running explicatory commentary. "Ordinary language is its own metalanguage" (Habermas 1972: 168; see also Sacks 1963; cf. Wittgenstein 1958). This brief excursus into CA however, gives a clue to the killer's "problem." The next action implicated by his announcement is the implied event contained in the announcement, namely some expression of his hatred, here shooting women dead. Indeed, insofar as the announcement is also a denunciation, it already contains an expression of his hatred. In any case, the implied next action is not conversation. Furthermore, his evident third action is suicide. These actions of his can be seen as attempts to remove the relevance of, and in part the opportunity for, others doing understanding checks where they can test any doubts they might have about what it is he is doing (see Cuff 1994: 37ff.). Thus, we have one basis for the accountability of his talk as an announcement.

But why might he suppose that others *might* mistake the meaning of his action without the accompanying announced description? If it is not that actions necessarily require "repair" to be intelligible, what "determinate alternative possible account" (Cuff 1994: 42) of the meaning of his action might the killer suppose he had specifically to counter? He tells us in his suicide letter: "Even if the Mad Killer epithet will be attributed to me by the media, I consider myself a rational erudite." He anticipated, quite correctly as it turned out, that he might be perceived as being mad for having killed fourteen strangers and then himself (see Jayyusi 1984: chap. 8, esp. p. 187). The relevance of an orientation to insanity on the part of reporters, respondents, and commentators is revealed in the frequent description of him or his actions in such terms as "crazy" (Dec 7 [1]), "a lunatic" (Dec 8 [2]), "insane," "insane people," "insanity," "sick minds" (Dec 8 [8]), "crazed gunman" (Dec 12 [1]), "crazed man" (Dec 12 [4]), and in the later report that "a majority of [polled] Canadians" see the murders as a "random violent act...by an insane person" (*KWR*, Dec 29). It is present, too, in the admonition not to see them in this way:

E67   It would be a great mistake, I think, to see this incident as some kind of freak accident, the act of a madman that has nothing to do with the society in which we live.[4] (Dec 8 [5])

E68   The appeal to mental illness is a familiar excuse. (Dec 12 [2])

It is most striking, however, in the use of "Oddly" in the following passage (from Extract 54 in chapter 3):

E69   Throughout the day, homicide detectives and journalists worked feverishly, trying to piece together more personal information on the man who systematically and calmly slaughtered 14 young women.
              Oddly, police could not turn up any evidence that Mr. Lepine had ever received psychiatric treatment.
              Mr Lepine was born...(Dec 9 [3]; emphasis added)

The danger of the insanity ascription for the would-be rational actor is that it removes the agency from the actor's acts; the acts become symptoms of the disease he is suffering from, and not the intended outcome of his motivated agency. And so he speaks, showing his "sanity" by giving a reason: "You're all a bunch of feminists. I hate feminists." As Watson (1990, 1983) has shown for "nigger" and "fag" and "tramp" (see also Wowk 1984) in his study of police interrogations of murder suspects, members may treat giving a category as a sufficient answer to a question asking for a reason for murder.

Insofar, then, as it names the category of his victims, the announcement can also be heard as reflexively doing the work of providing a reason for their victimization. As we argued above, this "methodological" step is crucial to his project. For if his victims are not available for observation-and-report *as* feminists, then the political identifiability of his action as against feminism is potentially lost. It would clearly not be sufficient to simply let his other actions speak for themselves. While his act of separating the women from the men is, observably and reportably, self-explicating—he wants the women, not the men—the problem is that this does not by itself make the "feminists" visible, feminist identity not being standardly or necessarily available to visual inspection alone. Moreover, while partitioning the classroom population by gender makes gender now a *relevant* descriptor in the setting (Schegloff 1991: 51), others such as "student" and "engineering students" are also relevantly available. Who then is he killing? Lépine solves the problem by naming out loud his victims as "women," who "are going to be engineers" and "are a bunch of feminists."

By naming his intended victims as feminists, Lépine "anonymizes" them; he speaks to them not as individual persons, with names, biographies, families, plans, and projects of their own; rather, he speaks categorially to them as *representatives* of feminism; he depersonalizes his victims and in so doing he politicizes them. His action, whilst concrete, is then also abstract since he kills not unique individual human beings but exemplars of categories in a political membership categorization device which comprises two membership categories: feminist "revolutionaries" and anti-feminist "counter-revolutionaries." Similarly, his task is to reveal, for his victims and for the general public or polity that constitutes his wider overhearing and political audience, that he is not acting as Marc Lépine per se but as a political actor, as a representative of a political stance. By invoking this device, Lépine categorizes both himself and his victims and in so doing he provides instructions for making his action rationally accountable as political.

The categorial logic of his reported speech is developed in a stepwise fashion. He categorizes his intended victims as "women," thereby explicating the relevance of gender as the basis of his act of separating them from the men, or confirming its visible relevance. He then attaches a predicate to that category, "You're going to be engineers," which names a second category, "engineers." This category is, however, one conventionally hearable as being at odds with, or at least standing in a problematic or contested relationship to, the gender category he has just used, being conventionally associated with the other category of the gender collection, "men." However, at this point in the utterance, these observations could be heard as no more than stating the obvious, namely that those to whom he speaks are (a) women and (b) student engineers. For this to be heard as objectionable requires that the historical association of men and engineering be invoked and the present connection between women and this traditional occupation be heard as disjunctive. The disjuncture is made available with the provision of a third category, "feminists," which is hearable as meaning "those women who would do men's jobs." Since these women in the classroom are going to be engineers, and engineering is a man's job, and only feminist women would take men's jobs, then these women must be feminists. This is what is unacceptable to him, and is at once the basis of his hatred and the subject of his hate. This conclusion gives him a political problem, which he chooses to address by killing these "women," "who are going to be engineers," who are thereby the hated "feminists."

The occasioned hearability of "feminists" as "those women who would do men's jobs" requires some further analysis. As we said at the outset of this section, the utterance, "You're all a bunch of feminists," stands to be heard as a *denunciation* (rather than a mere description or simply an announcement). It utilizes a conventional format for denouncing, "You're all a bunch of X," where X is a place holder for a collection of derogatory descriptors ("fags," "whores," "communists," "welfare bums"). Hearable denunciations provide for the relevance of a search to locate the "denounceable," the matter being denounced.[5] The preceding talk can provide resources for locating such a denounceable if the hearer can bring the categories named there ("women," "engineers") into a disjunctive relationship, the negative feature of which can be associated with the "denouncing" category ("feminists"). The status of the denouncing utterance *as* a hearable denunciation provides the warrant for that "search operation"; a successful finding reflexively confirms the status of the denunciation.

A significant warrant for our analysis of the killer's analysis is that it is reproduced in the reported analyses of witnesses. These include an employee "at a grocery store across the street from the killer's flat" (Dec 9 [3]) and, most strikingly, one of the victims who survived, Ms. Provost. It was she who attempted to talk the killer out of his apparent project (Dec 9 [1]). As Cuff (1994: 38–39) argues,

> to the extent that the materials do offer some display of how the parties are mutually orienting to one another in the ways their successive utterances are "chained" or "sequenced" or "locked into" one another, analysts do have some warrant for suggesting what hearings the parties are making and thus also the possibility of warrantably constraining the range of alternative possibilities.

Thus, Ms. Provost reportedly engages her task of contesting Lépine's category analysis by dissociating the category "women" and the activity "engineering" from the category "feminists." She supplies a replacement predicate for "feminists," namely, "ready to march on the streets to shout we are against men." And she recategorizes the women present as "students" who are "studying engineering" and are "intent on living a normal life," where that would, by inference, exclude "marching on the streets…" If the would-be killer is after feminists, she is saying, he is in the wrong place. The incident is reported as follows:

E70   *Don't have feelings of guilt, woman hurt in massacre urges her fellow students.*

Ms Provost said that when Mr. Lepine burst into her classroom, ordering the male students to leave and the women to remain, she tried to talk to him.

"When we were alone with him in the room… [*sic*] he said, "I am here to fight against feminism, that is why I am here."

"Maybe I was still not realizing fully what was happening, but I told him: 'Look, we are just women studying engineering, not necessarily feminists ready to march on the streets to shout we are against men, just students intent on leading a normal life.'" (Dec 9 [1])

He apparently takes no notice, or rather his response is to start shooting, displaying the non-negotiability of his analysis. As such, it may be noted that in contesting the analysis displayed in Lépine 's announcement, Ms. Provost demonstrates (unwittingly we presume) the danger of contesting the analyses that are exhibited by "offensive" others. This is because the grounds of contestation can be heard, as they are here, as confirming the analysis being contested in the first place. Thus, its contestability lies in the relation of "engineering" to the category "women." As an activity, "engineering" *can* be heard to exhibit feminism by virtue of its historical connection with men; that this student argues with Lépine on this point, apparently grounding her argument in the "unremarkable" fact that women are now becoming engineers and doing what were hitherto "men's jobs," only serves to confirm, for Lépine, that they are feminists since such a view would be predicated of feminists. Ironically, then, her protest, from his point of view, could be heard to reflexively contribute to the fire of his anti-feminism. Again, from Extract 54:

E71   Another employee said Mr. Lepine, 25, would sometimes make caustic comments about women. "He did not like feminists... women taking (traditional) men's jobs. He often spoke out against career women and he blamed his problem with getting into university on women (being accepted in such areas as engineering)." (Dec 9 [3])

The suicide letter

Lépine's suicide letter affords us further insight into how he defined his problem; it provides not only further instructions as to how to understand the murders as political but also makes accountable the political orientation of his suicide; the letter elaborates the analysis revealed and displayed in the announcement.

With reference to the first of these accountable actions—the killings—it is observable that in the first paragraph of his letter Lépine explicitly formulates his reasons as "political" and not, it may be noted, "economic" (and thereby possibly alluding to a conventional grammar of suicide). Indeed, it is politics he wants to be seen as engaged in, not random slaughter by a crazed gunman, or action for personal gain. He writes (from Extract 66):

E72   Would you also note that if I commit suicide today 89-12-06 it is not for economic reasons... but for political reasons. Because I have decided to send the feminists, who have always ruined my life, to their Maker.

The letter is unaddressed, but it addresses a reader. It asks the reader, for example, to "Forgive the mistakes," and it offers an apology for its abbreviated contents, "Sorry for this too brief letter." Who is the unnamed addressee? If politics defines his action, then presumably "the public" ("the people," "citizens," "government") are his addressee or audience, mediated by the police, the coroner, and "the media." As a counter-revolutionary terrorist he is not content for the functional significance of his crime to be the unintended outcome of the response to it, or for the wrong significance to be attached to it by whomsoever. He is his own political sociologist (see Hester and Eglin 1997e), and provides the "right" reading for all to see (see Mahood 1996: 367). Although he intends not to be available for the news interview, he knows that his act will make news and so he can address himself to "Anon," the citizenry, the public, the people who read the news. He speaks *to* the women in the classroom, but he speaks *for* an overhearing audience (Heritage 1985). And, providing he leaves survivors and/or the letter, they/we can find that he is talking to them/us (see Hester and Eglin 1997c: 35–38).

A few sentences later he invokes the example of [Denis] Lortie, whom he wishes he might have "precede[d] in a raid." Lortie had carried out an armed attack on the sitting Quebec National Assembly on May 8, 1984, killing three persons and wounding thirteen. The event received national media attention. It was reported at the time that he had sent to a local radio station a tape recording containing a statement that "he would destroy the Parti Québécois government for the "wrong" it had caused Francophones in Quebec and Canada" (*Canadian News Digest,* May 1–15, 1984: 3066). In invoking Lortie, then, Lépine explicitly invites comparison of his act with others that may be described as acts of political terror, or simply terrorism (cf. "suicide bombings"). That is to say, being a known-in-common person's name (Jayyusi, above), "Lortie" provides, via the consistency rule, for Lortie's and Lépine's acts to be heard as members of the same collection (political terror) and, by implication, for the common identity of the victims (political opponents).

The list of nineteen women's names attached to the suicide letter is accountable in a similar way as a means to make the category "feminist" available as a description of his victims. For one basis for their collectability is their public recognizability as "names of prominent Quebec feminists." The ready availability of these accountable inferences is, perhaps, one basis for the police refusal to release the letter and the list following the massacre; they may well have felt such an action would have constituted an invitation to others of Lépine's (and Lortie's) persuasion to have carried on his (or their) visibly unfinished project.[6]

We may say, then, that Lépine engages in the politics of terror. His co-selection of Lortie's and his own acts is reproduced by police and newspaper. To repeat and extend Extract 64:

E73   However, Mr. Duchesneau did highlight several points made by Mr. Lepine.
        "First, he mentioned he was doing this for political reasons. He said feminists have always ruined his life; that he wasn't too happy

in life, particularly in the last seven years; that he was rejected from
the Canadian Army because he was not sociable; and he made a
reference to Corporal Denis Lortie, saying he was only doing what
Mr. Lortie did."

(Mr. Lortie killed three people with a machine-gun in the Quebec National Assembly on May 8, 1984.) (Dec 8 [1])

Lépine's co-selection of himself and Lortie, and the reproduction of that co-
selection by police and newspaper, permit our generalization. Recall that our
question is: what provides for the reproduceability of such a politics? What
collections of categories are implicated in such politics and "how are they used
to determine whether there are eligible persons available" to terrorize? In short,
how may a political actor decide that murder-followed-by-suicide is a rational
course of action? Or, why the politics of terror and not that of the democratic
process? Just how Lépine may have come to seek to solve his political problem
in this particular way is the question we now want to take up.

To put it simply, his dilemma arises because he conceives the very institution that would be the vehicle for a democratic remedy to his problem, namely
the government, as the source of his problem. Lépine makes himself available
for comparison, we want to say, to the "angry white guys with guns" (Junas
1995) populating the anti-government "militias" in the United States. Noam
Chomsky characterizes their dilemma as follows:

> So take the angry white males who are maybe joining what they mistakenly
> call militias, paramilitary forces. These people are angry. Most of them are
> high school graduates. They're people whose incomes have dropped maybe
> 20% over the last fifteen years or so. They can no longer do what they think
> is the right thing for them to do, provide for their families. Maybe their
> wives have to go out and work. And maybe make more money than they do.
> Maybe the kids are running crazy because nobody's paying attention to
> them. Their lives are falling apart. They're angry. Who are they supposed to
> blame? You're not supposed to blame the Fortune 500, because they're
> invisible. They have been taught for fifty years now by intense propaganda,
> everything from the entertainment media to school books, that all there is
> around is the government. If there's anything going wrong, it's the govern-
> ment's fault. The government is somehow something that is independent
> of external powers. So if your life is falling apart, blame the government…
> All that you're hearing is that there's something bad about government, so
> let's blow up the federal building [referring to the Oklahoma City bombing].
> (Chomsky 1996: 83–84; see also Salutin 1997)

It may be argued in addition in our case that bombardment of the public
by anti-feminist propaganda made feminists a publicly available target of
recrimination for "angry white *males*," as Monique Bosco, Michele Landsberg,

and others have asserted. For example, the *Globe and Mail* reported, just three weeks before the massacre, that "it is not difficult to sense a more general feeling of resentment on the part of many male students towards the special measures undertaken to help women on campus, at Queens [University] and elsewhere."[7]

What Lépine considers to be the moral duplicity or hypocrisy of the "feminists"—"keep[ing] the advantages of women...while seizing for themselves those of men"—is made possible by the actions of government in legislating discriminatory benefits for women. Feminists and government are constituted as enjoying a tacit alliance in Lépine's argument. There is a formal parallel here with Sacks's case of the suicidal adulterous spouse who cannot turn for help to the R-prescribed category of other spouse. This is not because the other spouse is necessarily the source of the problem but because the adultery would necessarily be revealed and so occasion possible divorce rather than help (Sacks 1972: 58). Here Lépine, the political actor, paints himself into one corner by representing the political avenue for remedying his political problem as ending in another corner occupied, as it were, by the feminists.

When Lépine has committed the murders, the same analysis gives him grounds for suicide. Should he permit himself to be captured, he then faces the certain prospect of twenty five years, perhaps more, in prison at the government's pleasure. "Why persevere to exist if it is only to please the government?" he writes. Hence, turning to the government, turning to the democratic process (by becoming a member of the device "parties to the democratic process") is not an option. They (the government) do not provide a category with remedial potential. The government is undermined by the people he wishes to contest. Hence, to turn to government is to turn to the feminists—to the enemy. This, then, makes possible his terrorist activities; it enables him to step outside the democratic process because of the character of the government.

More formally, we may say that Lépine invokes an "immediately assymetric, standardized collectivity relational pair," namely government/citizens (or people) (Jayyusi 1984: 126; see also Coulter 1982). Each of the two collectivity pair parts stands in relationship to the other; indeed, the terms are inter-defined. The pair comprise what Sacks calls a "Pn-adequate" device; that is, the categories exhaust the population universe to which they are applied. Lépine occasions their oppositional, rather than complementary, feature. Via the predicate of "legislating social policy," which is a category-bound activity of the category "government," he can ally the beneficiaries of the policy in question to the benefactors. Insofar as "cheaper insurance, extended maternity leave" can be heard as government-legislated social policies benefiting women, and insofar as seeking such ends that benefit women can be seen as a category-bound activity of the category "feminists," then the categorizations "government" and "feminists" can here be read as in a tacit alliance of coincident interests.[8]

Moreover, Lépine clearly feels himself to be combatting a problem that exceeds the scope of domestic politics. Its domain is global, deeply historical, and, as well as being institutional, is ideological in nature. In the letter's last major paragraph he invokes the supra-national case of the gender difference built in to the organization of the Olympic Games. Here too, he claims, women's hypocrisy is evident. They would not want to break down *that* barrier, since they would end up losing out to men in all but the "graceful events." They are merely opportunistic, he states. The difficulty of opposing them is, additionally, a matter of coming to grips with arguments that are so extremely wrong, yet clearly holding public sway, that one can, as it were, only throw up one's hands in despair. Or go to war. From Extract 66:

E74 Thus, the other day, I heard they were honoring the Canadian men and women who fought at the frontline during the world wars. How can you explain then that women were not authorized to go to the frontline??? Will we hear of Caesar's female legions and female galley slaves who of course took up 50 percent of the ranks of history, though they never existed. [*sic*] A real Casus Belli.

The true record of major historical events is at stake. Indeed, by invoking classical and modern examples, he may be said to be defining the parameters of history itself. Like the subject of the examples themselves, there is nothing for it but war.[9] "Alea Jacta Est" [The Die Are Cast]. He quotes Caesar about to cross the Rubicon. Like the American militant anti-communist who is the subject of Sam Keen's noted social-psychological documentary, *The Face of the Enemy*, Lépine defines his circumstances and himself as being at war with an enemy. Going to war may be justified if one has exhausted the possibilities of the democratic process. Indeed, the preamble to the Universal Declaration of Human Rights states: "*Whereas* it is essential, if man is not to be compelled to have recourse, as a last resort, to rebellion against tyranny and oppression, that human rights should be protected by the rule of law"[10] (United Nations 1986 [1948]).

Lépine's method of waging war against the "tyranny and oppression" he represents himself as experiencing is that of terrorism. Category work is at the heart of terrorism. The method consists of terrorizing what can be seen as selected cases of the target category so that other category incumbents get the same message. Given the choice of terror as his political method, Lépine, we may say, had the problem of target selection. *Which* feminists would it be? We have already considered his problem of revealing his target category *as* feminists. But why choose the women engineering students at the Ecole polytechnique? ("Mr. Duchesneau said police still have not determined why Mr. Lépine chose the University of Montreal to carry out his vendetta against women" (Dec 8 [1]).) The Polytechnique had the virtue of being at hand.[11] "Students," as an occupational stage-of-life category, is anticipatory; it projects the future. Kill a student and you kill the future. For one intent on stopping the clock, for a counter-revolutionary, students are a meaningful target. For an anti-feminist, the category of women *engineering* students has the property of representing a bastion of male privilege (McCormack 1990: 32). In this sense, following Gaudet's argument (in note 9), the Ecole polytechnique is continuous with the Olympic Games, the Canadian armed forces and Caesar's legions. If women break through into this profession, one might argue, then the patriarchal game is lost (Smith 1992: 207). Through the murder of a sample of *this* category of persons, not only other women considering entering engineering but the whole feminist movement for equality in the workplace might be set back. Indeed, it is not necessary to speculate about this analysis for it was being made as early as the second day of reporting, as we noted in chapter 2 (see Extracts 13 and 14):

E75   "This is perhaps the first crime perpetrated against a whole sex. That's what this is all about," said University of Montreal criminologist, Jean-Paul Brodeur. (Dec 8 [2])

E76   It does not appear to be coincidence that Mr. Lepine chose the engineering school, one of life's remaining male enclaves being entered by women. ("What do I say to the parents," asked Louis Courville, dean of the engineering school, his voice breaking with emotion. "They send us their daughters who are then killed.") (Dec 8 [6])

Also:

E77   James Fox, a criminologist at Northeastern University in Boston who has co-wrote [*sic*] a book called Mass Murder: America's Growing Menace, agreed with Mr. Leyton about the uniqueness of the case.

    "This is the first case of someone who went on a rampage to revenge [*sic*] feminists," he said, adding that he found it interesting that the man chose an engineering school to wreak havoc.

    "Basically, he went to attack women who were attempting to take a traditional male job," he said, emphasizing that he does not want to be misconstrued as a male chauvinist.

    "If you want to get a lot of women, you should go to a nursing school or a school of social work. But...[*sic*] those are women doing what women are traditionally supposed to do.

    "What he went to do was to try to find women who were trying to take over men's jobs." (Dec 8 [10])

E78   Lepine killed the women he believed had taken his rightful place in a traditionally male-dominated profession, and who represented a general threat to men's powers and entitlements. (Dec 12 [2])

▼
CONCLUSION

Throughout the book we approach the media reporting and commentary on the Montreal Massacre as comprising a collection of stories or story lines. In chapter 3 we examined categorization-analytic features of the stories of crime, horror, tragedy, gun control, and the killer. In the following chapter we do the same for the story of violence against women. As we showed in the previous chapter, the story of the killer, that is the story *about* the killer, is developed at some length in the coverage we have studied. His character is described and details of his personal biography and social background ransacked in a search for motive. We pointed out how the "political angle" of his actions is reported but not pursued. Rather his killings are collected together with other mass murders, implying a rather different frame of interpretation than the one we have developed here.[12] We said that there is a preference exhibited in the categories of description employed in the coverage for viewing him as an instance of social and psychological pathology rather than as the "rational erudite" he sought to be.

This observation, however, might be thought to raise a problem for how our analysis here of "the killer's story" is to be taken. At the outset we said that we were concerned with the Montreal Massacre only as a *members' phenomenon*. Yet we have paid extraordinary attention to a story that is barely told in the collection comprising the Montreal Massacre. In what sense, then, is our analysis an analysis of a "members' phenomenon?" What is our warrant for telling a (partially) untold story?

In part, our warrant is the methodological one stated at the beginning of the chapter. Insofar as studies of criminal and deviant behaviour rarely address seriously the naturally occurring accounts of the criminals and deviants themselves, and insofar as such studies as have been done have tended to be post-hoc, decontextualized, quasi-causal reconstructions of such behaviour, and insofar as our own materials contain rare instances of a member of society, a "criminal," formulating explicitly the grounds of his actions in the course of doing them, then, we argued, they afford us a rich opportunity not only to conduct a study in membership categorization analysis, but to discover and investigate the "lost causes" of criminal and deviant behaviour as *accountable action.*

Our warrant also derives from our understanding of the Montreal Massacre *as* a members' phenomenon. Thus, it is possible to analyze the Montreal Massacre from a variety of members' points of view and in terms of various members' actions. In this chapter we have chosen to focus on the Montreal Massacre in terms of the articulated accounts of its perpetrator, whilst elsewhere in the book we consider this phenomenon as it is described, constituted, and commented upon in the work of various media personnel and other members of society. Indeed, with respect to these other contexts of membership categorization, it is rather unsurprising that the killer's own story is neither a major focus of attention nor taken particularly seriously *as an account.* Instead, it tends to be ignored and replaced with accounts external to his action. It is just such accounts we take up in the following chapters. As we shall see, such accounts are themselves recognizably predicated of the category members who produce them.

Finally, we note one particular aspect of the responses to Lépine's actions and its displayed intelligibility. Thus, just as Lépine's actions are avowedly and intelligibly *political*, so also are many of the responses. Understandably, much media reportage and commentary not only expressed their writers' moral outrage at Lépine's actions, it also engaged in political discussion in terms made relevant by the killings. Thus, Lépine's reported announcements at the scene and recovered suicide letter can be understood as addressing the general polity, or "us." That is, in invoking the immediately asymmetric, standardized collectivity relational pair of government/citizens (or people), he engaged others who might hear or read his words *as* fellow citizens. As his fellow citizens, the members of society (and those who speak "for" them in the media) have the category-tied entitlement to respond to him politically. As we indicate elsewhere, the media commentary and reportage that followed the Montreal Massacre accomplishes such a response via, for example, the engagement of avowedly feminist commentators to not only condemn Lépine's murders but also the wider "male violence against women" with which it can be collected. What is particularly interesting here, in terms of our approach, is how, in these media treatments, the Montreal Massacre as a members' phenomenon is conceived and categorized in and out of the self-same categorial resources deployed by Lépine himself. Lépine may have been "extreme" but he carved his actions out of the same materials—of oppositional, political categories—as did his respondents.

CHAPTER 5

The Story of Violence against Women

▼
INTRODUCTION

THE INITIAL CHARACTERIZATION of the massacre events—a "gunman" "with rifle" "at the University of Montreal" who "went on a rampage...killing 14 people before shooting himself dead"—makes them available as a set of potential story lines, or, we might say, "storyable" lines. "Offender/victim" provides for "police" and thus a crime story, in this case a homicide investigation. "Parties to a homicide investigation" include "witnesses to homicide" who, in a university setting ("at the University of Montreal"), make for a horror story. The setting provides for victims as "students" who also have "parents" and "friends," these categories affording a story of (private) tragedy; the number of dead, "14," and the setting being a public institution, provide for the response of "public figures," notably politicians, and so make for a "public disaster." That the killings are described as being done "with rifle" makes possible a "gun control story."

Other storyable lines are available in the initial characterization but are not developed into stories, at least in the coverage we have examined. Thus the killings are described as occurring "in Montreal." This provides for the relevance of the reactions of "Montrealers." While, as we shall see below, one article does report that "Everywhere on the streets, in restaurants and on open-line radio shows, Montrealers were discussing the tragedy..." (Dec 8 [2]), this line is not pursued in reportage or commentary. No story about, say, "violence in Montreal" is developed out of these events, though one commentator cautions readers to "watch now...for experts devising theories about the new faces of urban violence" (Dec 16 [1]). Notwithstanding columnist Lise Bissonnette's judgement that this was "the bloodiest crime in Quebec's modern history" (E0), and the report of witnesses that "the young gunman...spoke French" (E1), neither the *Globe and Mail* nor any other English-language press we read developed a story about, say, how the massacre betokens a "culture of violence" in Québécois society. That the killer is reported to have committed suicide ("shooting himself dead") does not become the occasion for working up a story on "suicide among young people." (Lépine's age is reported, and "25" is standardly regarded as "young" in claims-making about "youth suicide.") Indeed, as we saw in chapter 4, this is also true of the political character of the murders. Rather than the "killer's story," which *we* have reconstructed, we get "the story about the killer." As we argued in chapter 2 this is formally derivable by developing the predicate "searching for the offender's motive" which is tied to the category "police" in the device PHI. It is built, that is, out of the crime story.

If the "story about the killer" is written out of one half of the offender/victim pair in the crime story, it is perhaps not surprising that a story about the victims is produced out of the other half of the pair. What we want to address in this chapter is the *particular* story told about the victims, namely the "story of violence against women." We especially want to note two aspects of this story's development: the first is that it is only problematically present in the reportage of events; the second is that it is worked up in the response to and commentary on the events.

▼

THE PLACE OF THE KILLING OF *WOMEN* IN THE REPORTAGE

Let us say that in the news reportage there is a story line about the *killing of women,* that is to say a noticing that it was *women* who were killed. This story line runs through the following news articles—Dec 7 [1], [2]; Dec 8 [1], [2], [7], [12]; Dec 9 [1]; Dec 11 [1], [4], [5]; Dec 12 [1], [3], [4], [5]; Dec 13 [1], [2], [3]. We say "runs through" rather than, say, "is told in" because, although the victims are identified as women in all the reports, the articles, with one exception, are not in any strong sense *about* women or, indeed, the killing of *women.* That is, outside of the commentaries (which we take up below) and one news report, that the killer killed "women" is not consistently a topic of the reporting. This stands in contrast with the other stories outlined above. Crime (murder), horror, tragedy, gun control, and the killer are all explicitly referred-to and oriented-to topics of reporting. Despite the killer's reported announcements in speech and writing that he was killing women—(engineers)—feminists, *this* story is not one that clearly emerges. Indeed, to say this is partly to repeat the point of chapter 4, if from a different direction. And the non-emergence of this story is, fairly obviously, a category-based phenomenon.

Thus, although, as we said in chapter 2, in the first day's articles witnesses report (from E1; see also E23, E24) "'two and perhaps three *men*…shouting *anti-feminist* slogans,'" (emphasis added) and that

E79   "he (the man with the gun) ordered the men and women to separate sides of the classroom"

and

there were reports that the *gunman* shot mainly *women students*, but police would not release a breakdown of victims by gender

...

and the *man* appeared to be aiming mainly at *women* [and that] "I heard the gun*man* say: 'I want the *women*,'" [which] was confirmed by several other witnesses (Dec 7 [1]; emphasis added; see also Dec 7 [2]),

and that

E80   one student said the gun*man* threatened his cornered victims, shouting: "You're *women*. You're going to be engineers. You're all a bunch of *feminists*. I hate *feminists*!" (*KWR*, Dec 7 [1]; emphasis added),

nevertheless these observations are reported alongside others in which the gender of the victims is not topicalized. Thus (from E1):

E81   "All I know is that a *crazy guy* came in here and began shooting at *anything that moved*... It's our *friends* who have been killed."

...

"It was a *human* hunt... We were the quarry." (Dec 7 [1], emphasis added)

   Instead of "women," here we have "anything that moved," "friends," and "human hunt." Furthermore, two of the accounts of the separating of the women and men in the classroom are accompanied by witnesses' assessments that "We thought it was a joke" (Dec 7 [1]) and "It doesn't make sense" (Dec 7 [2]).

   This pattern is repeated on the second day. Thus, the lead article on the second day specifically notes that the victims were not only women but that the "killer's letter blames feminists," that it "contains [an] apparent hit list of 15 women" and "a vicious diatribe against women" (headline and first sentence, Dec 8 [1]), and that it "mentioned he was doing this for political reasons [and that] feminists have always ruined his life." Further on the article refers to "his vendetta against women." It contains, too, a report of a "reconstruction of the killing rampage" by the police, which makes plain that the intended targets were women (Dec 8 [1]; see E33). Nevertheless, the article also contains many other details about the inquiry gathered from the police news conference which is the chief source of the story. These refer to the discovery of the killer's identity, how he obtained the weapon, how he apparently knew in advance the layout of the school, how he was dressed, and so on. Gender and politics are not made accountable in the telling of *these* details. Rather they are blended with and constitute an aspect of the crime story.

Similarly, the second front-page story on the second day (see E17) qualifies "a man's … killing of 14 young women" with the adjective "senseless" both in the cited phrase from the first sentence and in the headline "Quebec mourns senseless deaths" (Dec 8 [2]). The article goes on to compile a variety of activities under this title, including flags flying at half-staff and the removal of Christmas decorations from the engineering school. Of those specifically referring to people, the first is the "tragedy" story of "teary-eyed students and … faculty … mourning their friends"; the second describes the "lone gunman, Marc Lepine" as one "who apparently hated women"; the third refers to "university officials" and "parents of the victims"; the fourth is a "candlelight vigil to mourn the loss of students and friends." The rest of the article does contain a number of explicit acknowledgements that the victims were women, but the acknowledgements are not unqualified:

E82   After the meeting, Mr. Mulroney told reporters: "This man singled out women in a completely criminal and insensitive fashion. It's an isolated incident, but it raises questions about violence in our society and about violence against women."
        …

        Everywhere on the streets, in restaurants and on open-line radio shows, Montrealers were discussing the tragedy, wondering what had triggered this man's vendetta against innocent women and questioning how this could have happened on the staid University of Montreal campus.
        …

        Helene David, psychology professor at the University of Montreal … predicted that many students, especially young women, will suffer from insomnia, nightmares and depression.
            "Some women will be afraid of going crazy because of the fear," she said.
            Dr. David said the vigil organized by women's groups yesterday evening was a good idea because it gave people the feeling that they were doing something about this senseless act.
            Dr. David is a member of the Corporation of Professional Psychologists of Quebec, which has set up a hot-line to counsel members of the general public who are troubled by the events, especially people who are "emotionally fragile."
            "As women we feel a deep, deep remorse that we can't bring these (14) women back," said Charlene Nero, one of the co-ordinators of last night's candlelight vigil. "But maybe there is something we can do to change society so this sort of thing does not have to happen again." She said the march was aimed at showing people "there is systemic oppression of women in society."

"The event did not happen in a vacuum," said Ms Nero, a spokesman for the Committee de Defence des Femmes, a group created in the wake of last year's rape of a young women [*sic*] at a McGill University fraternity.

"It was a lunatic who went on a rampage with the reinforcement of a lot of misogynist social values and a message that violence against women is okay," she said.

"This is perhaps the first crime perpetrated against a whole sex. That's what this is all about," said University of Montreal criminologist, Jean-Paul Brodeur. (Dec 8 [2])

That is, to take these paragraphs in E82 in turn, while this "man singled out women" which "raises questions about… violence against women," at the same time the killings are "an isolated incident" that also raise questions about "violence in society." While Montrealers are "wondering what had triggered this man's vendetta against innocent women" they are also "discussing the tragedy" and "questioning how this could have happened on the staid University of Montreal campus" (an allusion, we might say, to the horror story). While "especially young women, will suffer from insomnia, nightmares, and depression," and some "women will be afraid of going crazy because of the fear," Dr. David "urged anyone traumatized by the tragic event to seek help" and is "worried if someone who saw what happened had no reaction at all," predicting that "many students… will suffer from insomnia," etc. The counselling hotline is for "members of the general public… especially people who are 'emotionally fragile.'" While "as women we feel a deep, deep sense of remorse that we can't bring these (14) women back," and "there is systemic oppression of women in society" (for example, "last year's rape of a young wom[a]n…"), and the killer was reinforced "with a lot of misogynist social values and a message that violence against women is okay," nevertheless he "was a lunatic." Only in the last paragraph of the article is there an unqualified description of the killings as being "a crime perpetrated against a whole sex." In short, that women were the killer's intended victims is not paramount for witnesses, respondents, and reporter alike. It's a story line hedged with qualifications. It's a story line that "competes," as it were, with the stories of tragedy and horror. While there is concern for the massacre's effects on "women," there is also concern for "students," "members of the general public," "people," "someone," "anyone." While we get here the first mentions of "violence against women" we also get the more general, non-gender-specific formulation "violence in society." There's "systemic oppression of women" and "misogyn[y]," but there's also "luna[cy]."

A single news report *does* report the event as one about "women." It also comes on the second day of coverage, and runs as follows:

E83   *Hundreds in Toronto mourn killing of 14 women*
BY STEVIE CAMERON
The Globe and Mail

Weeping and holding one another for comfort, hundreds of women
and men—most of them students, professors, politicians and community activists—met yesterday before a statue of a crucified
woman on the University of Toronto campus to mourn the 14 women
who were murdered in Montreal on Wednesday night.

For many, the massacre was the brutal culmination of a season
of escalating violence and hatred directed at women, especially
toward those who are trying to make their way in professions—such
as engineering—which have traditionally not welcomed women.

They were horrified when Alice de Wolff, a Toronto organizer
for the National Action Committee on the Status of Women, told
them that among all the calls the organization's Ottawa office
received yesterday from women across Canada, there was a threatening one from an angry man who told them "that Marc is not alone."
(The women were murdered by a young man named Marc Lepine.)
(Dec 9 [7]).

It is noticeable that the actors in the story are referred to in terms of the gender device (women, men). That is, to be perfectly obvious, the women are not
only referred to as "women," but the men are referred to as "men." That this is
a category election, not simply a selection, is made visible through the provision of alternative descriptors ("students, professors, politicians and community activists") as, effectively, sub-categories of "women" and "men."

The rest of the article (a) quotes the gathering's speaker saying, "Remember the women who were killed because they were women," (b) introduces
the segments of women's reported speech that follow by saying, "again and
again, whether they were speaking during the brief service or just talking among
themselves, the women described the hostile society around them," and
(c) presents the segments themselves in which reference is made, for example,
to "a continuum of violence," "the issue of violence against women," and the
"fear women live with every day." These formulations, and others like them, are
considered in the second part of the chapter below. We mention them here to
note that in keeping with the categorization of its subjects as "women," the
article formulates the "14 women who were murdered" in terms of (a problem
called) "violence against women." While the focus on "women" clearly distinguishes the story it tells as a story about the killing of women (and not one
about horror, tragedy, etc.), it still misses the story told by the killer himself, what
a later commentator calls "Marc Lepine's political killing of women" (Dec 12 [2]).

Let us note, too, one interesting piece of categorial work that marks this
report as itself hearably "feminist." It occurs in the opening two phrases where

activities predicated of R-based categories are attached to the gender categories of "women" and "men." That is, while we have indicated in chapters 2 and 3 how the story of tragedy is located in part in terms of the organization of relationship pairs relevant to the search for help, here the writer associates R-tied predicates, namely "weeping" and "holding one another for comfort," with membership categories not conventionally members of R, namely "women" and "men." The description invites the reader, as it were, to see the "tragedy" as a matter relevant to the "relationship" between woman and woman, man and man and, presumably, woman and man. As Sacks argued for "hotrodder" (as a young person's preferred self-description to the other-description "teenager"), revolutionary social change is (at least) a matter of changing the categories of everyday life: "there's an order of revolution which is an attempt to change how it is that persons see reality" (Sacks 1992a: 398; 1979). Stevie Cameron, the reporter, takes her cue from Marc Lépine, the counter-revolutionary, who treats a category ("women") as a group. This returns to our conclusion in chapter 4, and anticipates a topic about which we have more to say in chapter 7.

▼

THE PROFESSIONAL COMMENTARY: THE MURDERS AS "VIOLENCE AGAINST WOMEN"

In the section above we have considered the problematic status of the killing of women as a story line in the reporting. We now turn to the explicit formulations of the murders contained in the "professional commentary." In the period of coverage under scrutiny here, such commentary came in the form of editorials, op-eds, columns, and interviews reported as news stories, as follows: an editorial entitled "Why were women in the gunsight?" (Dec 8 [3]); an op-ed by Emil Sher, "a Montreal writer," entitled "The Massacre in Montreal: Speaking about the unspeakable" (Dec 8 [4]); an op-ed by Diana Bronson, "a Montreal journalist who wrote the following commentary for CBC's *Morningside* program," entitled "A time for grief and pain" (Dec 8 [5]); a column by Michael Valpy entitled "Systematic slaughter is without precedent" (Dec 8 [6]); interviews with Elliot Leyton, "an anthropologist at Memorial University in Newfoundland," and James Fox, "a criminologist at Northeastern University in Boston," entitled "Mass murders not increasing, Canadian anthropologist says" (Dec 8 [10]); a column by Stevie Cameron entitled "Our Daughters, Ourselves," featured on the front page of the "Focus" section of the Saturday paper (Dec 9 [5]); a column by John Allemang entitled "Violence and anger" (Dec 9 [6]); a second column by Michael Valpy entitled "Litany of social ills created Marc Lepine" (Dec 11 [3]); a second interview with Elliot Leyton, additionally described as "A Canadian expert on mass murders" and "author of *Hunting Humans: A Study of Serial Killers and Mass Murderers*," entitled "Slayings deal blow to gender relations, murder expert says" (Dec 11 [4]); an op-ed by Melanie Randall, "a doctoral student in political science at York University and a researcher-activist in the field of women and violence," entitled "Men cannot know the feelings of fear" (Dec 12 [2]); a third column by Michael Valpy entitled "Risk of murder linked to non-domestic roles" (Dec 12 [6]); a column by Lise Bissonnette entitled "The self-centred hype of Montreal massacre" (Dec 16 [1]); and an editorial entitled "Grieving together" (*KWR*, Dec 12 [2]).

Throughout our corpus there's more brief comment from a variety of sources included in news stories about particular events (as we have indicated already in the first section of this chapter), or in one or two of the columns already cited; such sources include an anthropologist, three psychologists, five sociologists, a criminologist, a political scientist, spokespersons for women's organizations, spokespersons for pro-feminist men's organizations, two deans of engineering, representatives of engineering associations, a rabbi, Anglican ministers, a university chaplain, government and university officials responsible for women's issues, a lawyer, well-known feminists, politicians, counsellors, newspaper editors, university presidents and other administrators, students, and student organization representatives.[1]

We will not attempt an analysis of the entirety of this corpus of commentary. Instead, we will concentrate on the major story carried in and as the commentaries. Thus, in previous chapters we identified the "stories" told and embedded in the newspaper reports (and, in the case of the story about the killer, running into some of the commentary also). In the section above we have identified the problematic story line of the "killing of women" as it can be found in the reportage. In the commentaries that immediately followed, and that in some cases were coincident with the reportage, the overarching story was that of "male violence against women" and, by extension, a story of "men and women" and "male-female relations." That is, the story in the commentaries was fundamentally not only a crime story about the offender and his victims but about what the murders "represent." In the remainder of this chapter we will consider this "story" contained and carried in and as the commentaries' explicit formulations with respect to showing/finding the *collection* to which the killings belonged—that is, what kind of killing it was. As will be seen this became a contested matter, a matter of dispute. In the next two chapters we will examine the story insofar as it comprises, respectively, *explaining/accounting for* the occurrence of the killings, and formulating the *consequences* of the killings.[2]

Collecting the action

If the killer speaks directly and categorially to his victims and indirectly to the public, media commentators respond indirectly to him and categorially on behalf of his victims. Furthermore, these responses are recognizably moral-political and condemnatory in character.[3] These responses not only condemn the massacre itself, they also condemn what the killer, his action, and his avowed motivation *represented*. If Marc Lépine prefaced the murders by denouncing feminists, then the subsequent commentary responded to him by denouncing violence against women (see E102 below). The commentaries are ordered therefore in categorial terms. Indeed, it is unsurprising that this should be so, since Lépine himself makes relevant such a categorial response both by his selection of "women" and "engineering students" as his victims and also by his transformation of them into "feminists." If Lépine provides an account for, and thereby one way of making sense of, his killings, then a major preoccupation of the commentaries which followed is with providing an account that not only makes sense of his murderous acts but also of the account that he provides for them.

The murders are not treated as murders *tout court*. Rather, the murders are *abstracted* and *generalized*. In the manner of a "Chinese Box," they are transformed from a collection of murders into an instance of a "bigger problem" that they *represent*, namely, "violence against women." Notice that this involves two logical procedures, first abstracting the offence from "murder" to the more inclusive category of "violence," and second generalizing the victims from the "fourteen women" to "women." This categorial expansion of the event, together with its assigned status as a "problem," is in turn encapsulated by some commentators within "wider" collections, such as "male chauvinism" and "misogyny." This again involves further abstraction: "violence" is abstracted to include perceivedly harmful but *physically* non-violent, acts and also attitudes, and "women" is abstracted to the "female sex or gender." Abstracting and/or generalizing the category of victims is evident in the following assertions (the first from E13):

E84   "This is perhaps the first crime perpetrated against a whole sex. That's what this is all about," said University of Montreal criminologist, Jean-Paul Brodeur. (Dec 8 [2])

E85   We haven't had this happen before, where a mass murderer chose "the Auschwitz ramp"—as Jean-Paul Brodeur, head of the university's International Centre for Criminology, put it—for half the human race. (Dec 8 [6])

Abstracting the offence occurs in such instances as follow:

E86   Senator Lorna Marsden, a University of Toronto sociologist specializing in women's issues, characterized the Montreal murders as the historical continuity of violence against women. (Dec 8 [6])

E87   Bob Wadden, a member of the Toronto Men's Forum, said: "This massacre in Montreal was not created by a madman as the media are plugging it. This sort of thing happens every day… [*sic*] women are abused every day." (Dec 11 [4])

A number of commentators list the co-members of this collection. In the first of the examples that follow, by Diana Bronson, "a Montreal journalist," the collecting work is done in terms of a formulation of "what he represents."

E88   It does not matter that the man who decided to kill 14 women—and he clearly did decide to do that—killed himself afterward; it is not of him I am afraid. I am afraid of what he represents, of all the unspoken hatred, the pent-up anger that he expressed. Hatred and anger that is shared by every husband who beats his wife, every man who rapes his date, every father who abuses his child, and by many more who would not dare. (Dec 8 [5])

E89   Melody McLoughlin Marratto, a chaplain at St. Jerome's College, told the crowd that "for the incest survivor, the battered women, the rape victim, what happened in Montreal can only be understood as a symbol of the larger problem of men's violence against them." (*KWR*, Dec 14)

In addition to listing the co-members of the collection "violence against women," the following cases partially *order* them. Melanie Randall writes:

E90   But how different is Marc Lepine's violence from that of the many husbands who batter and sometimes kill their wives, or from that of rapists who stalk women on the street or break into their homes? ...The only difference between his crime and less visible ones is the *scale* of the violence and its very *public* nature. (Dec 12 [2]; emphasis added)

E91   "There have been the panty raids, but there are also assaults. The university is not taking this seriously. The university doesn't take anything seriously unless fund-raisers threaten not to give money over something."
       What some university administrators may see as harmless fun is, in fact, part of a *continuum to* [sic] *violence,* said Lois Reimer, the University of Toronto officer responsible for the status of women. "It's the *pranks through to violence syndrome,*" she said. (Dec 8 [7]; emphasis added)

E92   And men need to focus on learning to communicate their painful feelings, said Richard Clarke, co-ordinator of the family violence treatment program at the Guelph-Wellington Counselling Centre.
       "Marc Lepine, in his *extreme* behaviour is at the *extreme* end of what a lot of men do with their lives, which is they get isolated, and contain their pain and their fear, to the point where it comes out explosively and aggressively." (*KWR*, Dec 18; emphasis added)

E93   The massacre in Montreal
Speaking about the unspeakable
BY EMIL SHER
Mr. Sher is a Montreal writer.
MONTREAL

THE WANTON SLAUGHTER of 14 women at the University of Montreal has taken male violence against women to *unimaginable
lengths*.

...

We discuss the weather or last night's game with fluid ease, but
when it comes to rape, assault and battery, we stall. (Dec 8 [4])

The answer, then, to Melanie Randall's rhetorical question in E90 is given by her
and, as it were, by the others quoted, as being that Lépine's offence is different
from the other forms of violence against women only in its "scale" on "a continuum" from "pranks through to violence": it is more "public," or "extreme," or
indeed "unimaginable" in its position on that scale or continuum. The categories of violent act that comprise this collection are, then, arranged position-
ally, higher and lower, relative to each other, in terms of the dimension of the
degree of violence perpetrated against women.[4]

Furthermore, the collection "male violence against women" includes what
are recognizable as various "myths" about male-female relations, and in particular, a collection of "mythical" predicates of women and a collection of predicates of "male chauvinistic men." Thus, in a parody of "male chauvinist man,"
Sher continues:

E94   Do men have nothing to say about violence against women? We do.
"Assaulted women like being beaten," a police officer said in a study
prepared by the New Brunswick Council on the Status of Women,
perpetuating a dangerous myth before launching another.

"I tell them, 'You like it since you stay with him.'"

He continues: "And I tell the guy to hit harder. If they go to court,
these men have no chance. There is no justice. Feminists and Stalinists have influence on the judges."

Clearly, at least one Manitoba judge has yet to be swayed by
these "feminists and Stalinists," or by any other women branded with
the labels we reach for when feeling defensive. He condoned the
behaviour of a man who had pleaded guilty to hitting his wife.

"How does a person admonish his wife," he asked, "if she goes
out on the town with other people... when she should have been
home looking after the children or cooking, or whatever else she is
expected to do?"

What we expect them to do is to talk about violence against
women as though it were "their" problem and theirs alone, as though

men have nothing to contribute to the issue other than a well-placed fist.

And we expect women to keep things in perspective, to be reasonable. To point fingers is unladylike. When we hear words such as "misogyny" we counter with "hysterical," dismissing women's concerns as the shrill protests of feminists and castrating lesbians. Or maybe "it's just that time of month."

WORSE we try to defuse anger with misguided humour. Why talk seriously about violence against women when we can joke about it? When the Canadian Federation of Students launched an anti-date-rape campaign with the slogan "No means no," students at Queen's University were swift to respond with versions of their own, all in the spirit of a "good joke"—"No means tie me up," "No means kick her in the teeth." (Dec 8 [4])

These myths, then, are themselves part of the collection, part of the problem, of "male violence against women." Continuity with other acts of male violence is also accomplished by referring to the collection "weapons which are used in violence against women." Thus:

E95   The author of the Montreal massacre used a semi-automatic rifle, but that is only one deadly part of the arsenal turned daily against women. Fists are still the preferred weapons in domestic disputes— marginally less violent than firearms, but as ugly and sometimes fatal. There is a wide range of psychological artillery. Some was observed, to our considerable national shame, in the House of Commons where, in 1982, Margaret Mitchell, a New Democratic Party MP, was greeted with jokes and laughter when she raised the subject of wife-beating.

More recently, we were given a discouraging glimpse of contemporary campus attitudes at Queen's University in Kingston, Ontario. When female students launched a "No means no" campaign against date-rapes, male students responded with a contemptuous "No means more beer" placard. (Dec 8 [3])

As indicated earlier, for some commentators, the killings themselves, and the problem of male violence against women that they represent, are subsumable under the wider collections of "male chauvinism" and "misogyny":

E96   This is a society that still moves with reluctance, and sometimes with bitter resistance, towards acceptance of the idea that women are entitled to equality in areas formerly dominated by men. Despite the changes that have been made—or possibly because of them— there is fertile ground for the misogynist or male chauvinist.

The author of the Montreal Massacre.... (Dec 8 [3])

E97   FOURTEEN WOMEN are dead for one reason: they are women. Their male classmates are still alive for one reason: they are men. While gender divides us in thousands of ways every day, rarely are the consequences of misogyny so tragic.
...

Now there is little that is comforting to say to women. It is a time for grief for all of us; grief for those who have died, and pain at being reminded of how deep misogyny still runs in our society. (Dec 8 [5])

E98   "Basically, he went to attack women who were attempting to take a traditional male job," [criminologist James Fox] said, emphasizing that he does not want to be misconstrued as a male chauvinist. (Dec 8 [10])

E99   **Slayings deal blow to gender relations, murder expert says**

A Canadian expert on mass murderers says the slayings of 14 women at the University of Montreal last week is "a grievous blow" to relations between men and women.

Elliot Leyton, an anthropologist at Memorial University in Newfoundland, said the killings demonstrate how male chauvinism threatens women's lives.
...

Gordon Cleveland [a member of the pro-choice group Men for Women's Choice] called for a royal commission to study violence against women in Canada. He said that the killing has "lifted the veil on one of society's collective secrets—widespread misogyny." (Dec 11 [4]).

E100 Anglican priest Stuart Summerhayes confessed feeling shame for "being a man" during a candle-lit church memorial service Saturday for the 14 Montreal women slain by a gunman yelling he hated feminists.
...

The service was alternately led by Rev. Elizabeth Macdonald, the minister of the church, and Summerhayes, of Cambridge.
...

"and I have the additional feeling of shame, of being a man, because I know this incident was evidence of a pervasive feeling in society among men that can only be described as misogyny."

Misogyny is the term for hatred of women. "I don't think that's too strong a word," Summerhayes told the gathering.
...

In an interview after the service, Macdonald said she agreed that the killings were evidence of misogyny in society. (*KWR*, Dec 11 [3])

Like Summerhayes, other commentators categorize the killings as an expression of "hatred of women." For example, John Villinga, president of the University of Waterloo's engineering society, speaking at a memorial service for victims of the massacre, is quoted as follows:

E101   "The same hatred and ignorance which drove Marc Lepine to his despicable act is alive and well in many sane men, men who should realize that they are no better than the murderer, that their sanity is the only thing preventing their hatred from springing out in gruesome display." (*KWR*, Dec 14)

Finally, the related concept of "deep resistance" to gender equality is expressed in the following extract:

E102   More than 300 grieving students, faculty and staff at the University of Guelph heard violence against women denounced Friday at a memorial ceremony for the 14 women students slain in Montreal.

U of G president Brian Segal urged those present to put their commitment to equality for women into action as they mourn.

"Both the roles of women in our society and the relationships between men and women have changed. We must not deny that this reprehensible act is a manifestation of deep resistance to expressions of the equal worth of women and men," Segal said. (*KWR*, Dec 9 [1])

The inclusion of Lépine's actions in the collection "violence against women" is, we suggest, an unsurprising occurrence, not so much because this particular interpretation can be heard as predicated of journalists and commentators but because interpreting the significance (and standardly the moral-political significance) of events is an activity bound to the category of journalist/commentator. That is, the task of the commentator is *not* to do reportage; in the division of media labour that task is tied to and indeed left to the reporters. It is, then, the task of commentators to *do something with*, to formulate, what has been reported. For this membership category, providing "editorial comment," "insight," "discussion," and "opinion" is a category-bound activity. Of course, any event is at least in principle open to various interpretations and so, again unsurprisingly, an alternative interpretation duly appeared on cue.

Alternative formulations: the organization of categorial dispute

Just as the explicit formulations constituting the "story" of "male violence against women" and more generally "male chauvinism" and "misogyny" appear on cue, so also does an "alternative" story. This alternative story categorizes the story of male violence against women as the "feminist" account, thereby providing for the hearability of its own story as the "non-feminist" account.

The dispute between these two "versions" of the murders is then carried in the commentaries as a further "story," which is organized in terms of the standard journalistic device, the "debate." That is, the dispute between feminist and non-feminist accounts of the murders is mapped onto the debate contrast class, or format. It is the dispute about the "correct" formulation of the murders, which then becomes the story carried in and as further reportage and commentary.[5]

Before being developed in the work of commentary, the dispute is first of all reported. Thus, half way through an article leading with "more than 300 grieving students, faculty and staff at the University of Guelph heard violence against women denounced Friday at a memorial ceremony for the 14 women students slain in Montreal," the reporter writes:

E103 People across the country have thrown themselves into debate, on radio, television and everywhere crowds gather, over whether the massacre in Montreal is an isolated incident by one deranged man, or a symptom of a wider issue in which feminism is so deeply resented by some men that women cannot feel safe. (*KWR*, Dec 9 [1])

Three days later:

E104 **Mourners see better world**
Massacre debated as 14 buried

... But Marc Lepine's brutal slaying of 14 women Wednesday night has opened another wound in Canadian society—one that is more likely to fester than heal for a long time to come.

Across the country, a debate is raging over the implications of the gunman's act, and it is causing growing divisions between women who call themselves feminists and those who do not; between men and women; and even among men.

Two main opinions have polarized the issue. For some the shooting is viewed as an isolated act of a madman. For others, particularly feminists, it is an extreme example of the often violent male treatment of women woven into the fabric of Canadian life. (*KWR*, Dec 12 [1])

The news article then proceeds to collect and cite instances from different parts of the country of the contrast or rift between "feminist" and "non-feminist" versions. These include the four female engineering students who protest to a female instructor following her speech at a vigil that the death has been "made into a feminist issue," the "drown[ing] out by boos from male and female students in the crowd" of a woman who spoke at a vigil and "generalized about men's hatred for women," and the implicit contrasts built into reports of a "scuffle [that] broke out at the end of a vigil ... when a group of women tried to prevent a man from addressing the crowd," and of "men who wanted to attend a vigil … [being] told it was for women only." (*KWR*, Dec 12 [1])

The non-feminist view is contained, moreover, in reports that "some men" are "unable" to see the continuity between the murders and other forms of male violence, misogyny, and male chauvinism. Such a claim, of course, neatly encapsulates a mundane version of the significance of the murders, namely that they are continuous with other forms of male violence *independent* of their recognition or (in this case) non-recognition (see Pollner 1974a; 1974b; 1978; 1987; Eglin 1979b; Hester 1990; Hester and Eglin 1992: 128–130, 212–216). For example, at a memorial service at Wilfrid Laurier University, where an issue about "panty raids" had arisen two months before, Sharon Severinski, "a graduate student in social work,"

E 105　　said many men on campus still can't see a connection between the panty raids, attitudes toward women in society, and the shooting in Montreal.

　　　　　　The shooting has had an impact on some men, especially those who were already trying to improve gender relationships, she said.

　　　　　　"But for other men, it hasn't changed anything. Many still don't connect this with what we saw the panty raids to be, a form of violence against women. They still see it as good clean fun, just a bunch of people having a good time." (*KWR*, Dec 13 [1])

Likewise:

E 106　　**59% call massacre only random act, poll finds**

　　　　　　A majority of Canadians say they see no connection between the Montreal massacre of 14 women and violence against women in general, according to a poll released today.

　　　　　　Six in 10 say that the massacre, in which the gunman raged against "feminists," was a random act by an insane person and that it has nothing to do with attitudes in society.

　　　　　　But close to four in 10 Canadians do view the Dec. 6 massacre as a symptom of widespread male violence toward women, according to the poll by the Angus Reid Group. (*KWR*, Dec 29)

In the non-feminist version, what the murders are *said* to represent is itself organized in categorial terms, and is analyzed as such by its proponents. Thus, the *representation* of the killings as "male violence against women," "male chauvinism" and "misogyny," the *explanation* of the killings as a product of a "mad male chauvinist" in a social context of widespread misogyny and the *formulation of the consequences* of the murders as "reminding," "affirming," and "demonstrating" the pervasive "problem of male violence against women" (matters we deal with in chapters 6 and 7) are treated as *predicated* of a partic-

ular membership category, namely "feminists." Opponents of the feminist formulations accuse the feminists of having "hijacked" the murders for their own
political purposes. They take issue with these explicit formulations of the feminists. The alternative view is offered in the following editorial:

E 107   Grieving together

> The brutal slaying of 14 women at the University of Montreal is a
> cause of nation-wide grief and mourning. But ascribing a general
> motive to such an irrational act does a disservice to the memory of
> the victims and increases the anguish of their families and friends.
>
> The national outpouring of grief has been interrupted by those
> who would have all men accept blame for the murderous actions of
> one crazed man. Men have been excluded from vigils and rallies on
> a presumption that they have no business there.
>
> Counter-productive feminism ignores that the victims had
> fathers, brothers and boyfriends who suffered a terrible loss, too. It
> ignores the reality that all grieve when 14 lives are extinguished in
> wanton violence, whether the victims are women, children—or men.
>
> Inverted chauvinism deflects attention from the terror that
> erupted. Turning horror into a bandwagon will not help the cause of
> women or end the real violence too many suffer. With 14 now laid
> to rest, those who have usurped the high ground of mourning should
> bury prejudice. For the sake of shared humanity, let us join to ensure
> such tragedy does not occur again. (*KWR*, Dec 12 [2])

Several organizational features of this (and other like commentary) may be
noted. First, there is dispute with regard to the collection to which the murders
belong, in terms not only of the categorization of offence and victims but of the
offender too. Thus, whereas in the feminist version the offence (the murders)
is abstracted to "male violence against women," in the non-feminist version the
abstracting is "redoubled" (cf. Watson 1990: 266–267) so as to make of the
offence an instance of violence per se or, rather, an instance of the collection
"crimes against humanity." The feminist collection, then, is deemed to privilege a particular membership category, namely women, and thereby to implicate the relevance only of those violent offenders who also happen to be men.
For the non-feminist collection, other categories of victims and offenders are
made available. Thus, Gwen Landolt, "spokesman for REAL Women of Canada,"

E 108   doesn't view the shooting as a feminist issue—an example of phys-
>   ical abuse women and children suffer daily at the hands of men—
>   but as one incident from a violence-ridden society, in which men
>   brutalize men and children beat up other children. (*KWR*, Dec 12 [1])

Second, the non-feminist view accuses its feminist counterpart of *over-
generalization*. That is, feminists are accused of treating violence, chauvinism,

and misogyny as predicates of "all" men rather than as predicated of a limited subsection of the category. In fact, it is implied, there may be no generalizable offence insofar as the offender is characterized as "one crazed man." Third, feminists are accused of *obscuring and ignoring* significant dimensions of the phenomenon. Thus, as we observed earlier, the recognizably "feminist" character of at least one news report about the murders involves in part the attachment of R-based predicates to the gender category of "women," such that women, in co-category incumbency with the victims, can recognizably and properly "grieve," "weep," "mourn," and so forth, activities routinely predicated of "family members" and other "intimates." In the above commentary, this version and the entitlements it provides for is set in competition with two other collections which, according to the writer, are ignored by feminists, namely, R on the one hand ("fathers, brothers, and boyfriends") and "humanity" ("all") on the other. The feminist usurpation of the *tragedy* is evident in this claimed entitlement to, and apparent exclusive "ownership" of, the predicates of members of R. Moreover, the editorialist avers, this view fails to accord proper appreciation to the *horror* and *terror* of the event. By privileging the stories of crime, horror, tragedy (private and public), and the deranged killer, the commentary can be heard as "counter-revolutionary" insofar as it can be heard to challenge the feminist story of the murders as violence against women, and of what may be done and by whom in response to them.

The story of dispute is carried not only in reports and commentary containing the non-feminist alternative, it is carried also in feminist responses to their critics. The non-feminist alternative story is characterized in the feminist response as a vehicle for "an anti-feminist backlash." Thus, the "backlash" itself becomes "news" and a topic of commentary. In the *Globe and Mail* this occurs first on December 12, in a major op-ed by Melanie Randall.

E 109   **"Men cannot know the feelings of fear"**
Yet an anti-feminist backlash has been intensified
by the massacre in Montreal
by Melanie Randall

Ms Randall is a doctoral student in political science at York University and a researcher-activist in the field of women and violence.

WE HAVE SEEN an outpouring of grief, rage and despair as Canadians struggle to come to terms with the shooting of 14 women last week in a Montreal engineering school. Thirty-five hundred mourners attended a funeral service for nine of the victims yesterday.

There has also been an agonizing attempt to make sense of why a lone gunman would walk into a classroom, separate the men from the women and kill only the women.

The result has been a national crisis of conscience. Women across Canada are speaking of the massacre as both symbolic and symptomatic of a society that creates misogyny and tolerates it.

The social context of the crime has been analyzed in much of the media coverage, and yet the slaughter has also fanned the flames of a seething anti-feminist backlash directed against feminism as a social movement and against individual women who identify themselves (or are identified by others) as feminist.

It has created the conditions in which many consider it "inappropriate" and "extremist" to view the killings—the deliberate and brutal actions of one man—as an act of violence against women. It has made it seem dangerous for women to speak out as feminists.

This backlash comes in direct response to the significant social advancement women have made over the past few decades. And in relation to Marc Lepine's political killing of women, it is emerging in a number of distinctly identifiable ways.

The first is the denial that this shooting must be recognized primarily as an act of violence against women.

...

THE SECOND form of the backlash is found in the theory that this was the inexplicable and random act of a madman.

...

The backlash's third and less thinly veiled form is an explicit hostility towards women, especially feminists. (Dec 12 [2])

Randall counters the re-collecting work of the non-feminists and reasserts the applicability of the "male violence against women" version of events on the grounds, first, that the victims were, after all, *women*, and, second, that all "females" share co-membership of the category "victims." As she puts it, the non- or anti-feminist view "challenged women's right to grieve, to rage at the vulnerability and terror we feel as a condition of being female."

In the feminist response it is not only the murders that are to be included in the collection of "male violence against women"; so also is the "backlash" itself. Or, since the article is not entirely clear on this, the backlash is to be added to the collection "misogyny," of which "violence against women" is already a part. Randall's article continues as follows:

E110 The backlash's third and less thinly veiled form is an explicit hostility toward women, especially feminists. It is being claimed that "radical feminists are using this tragedy as a platform against men." This view was echoed in a news item broadcast last Thursday on CFPL-TV in London, Ont., in which the reporter commented that a rally held at the University of Western Ontario should not have been "a vehicle for feminist diatribe."

The following morning it was demonstrated graphically in a letter read by host Peter Gzowski on CBC Radio's Morningside program. Its male author accused the CBC of pandering to feminists, and called Mr. Gzowski a "wimp" for his respectful attention to feminist analyses of a wide variety of issues. In other words, real men don't like feminists.

Such sentiments are chillingly evident in graffiti on the uwo campus calling for people (men?) to "kill feminist bitches" and in the much-publicized response of male students at Queen's University to the feminist, "no means no" campaign against rape. On the weekend, CBC Radio's Sunday Morning also reported that, the day after the Montreal massacre, male students at Queen's entered classrooms, pointed their fingers at female students and pretended to pull imaginary triggers.

What are we to make of this? How can we possibly account for this chilling display of threatening and hateful behavior unless we grapple with some men's need to assert their own power through invoking utter panic and terror in women?

The universities are a microcosm of society as a whole. The same trend is seen in police officers who blame victims for being sexually assaulted and in judges who accuse sexually abused 3-year-old girls of being "sexually aggressive." It is seen in the outright misogyny of so-called "father's rights" activists who challenge women in court for child custody and minimize the crimes of rape and other forms of sexual abuse. It is seen in the resistance to non-sexist language and to feminists' insistence that it be used. It is seen in terrorist acts against women's services (such as the 1983 firebombing of the Toronto Women's Bookstore), the violence committed against abortion clinics, and the harassment of the women who attempt to enter them.

It is also seen in the resistance to such programs as employment equity and equal pay legislation, which are intended to correct men's unspoken affirmative-action systems, which have been advancing their interests for hundreds of years. (Dec 12 [2])

That is to say, the backlash is categorized as "explicit hostility toward women, especially feminists." As such, it is then co-collected with publicly broadcast comments opposing particular expressions of feminist analysis, campus graffiti calling "for people (men?) to 'kill feminist bitches,'" Queen's University students' responses to the "no means no" campaign, and the reported incident after the massacre when male students pointed fingers at female students and pretended to pull imaginary triggers. The commentator asks how to make sense of this and then does so with the following formulation: "it is a chilling display of threatening and hateful behavior." Again, it is claimed that some men "need to assert their own power through invoking utter panic and terror in women."

Randall goes on to argue for pervasiveness of "violence against women," listing the following as categories of acts which "assert men's power": police officers who blame victims for being sexually assaulted, judges who accuse sexually abused 3-year-old girls of being "sexually aggressive," the "outspoken misogyny" of so-called "father's rights" activists who challenge women in court for child custody, the resistance to non-sexist language and to feminists' insistence that it be used, terrorist acts against women's services, the violence committed against abortion clinics, and the harassment of the women who attempt to enter them. As the author concludes, "What happened in Montreal cannot be understood as anything other than a deliberate and brutal expression of the larger problem of men's violence against [women]."

The dispute, then, is organized and presented in terms of an argument about the categorization of the murders: do they belong to collection A ("violence against women") or collection B ("violence" in general)? Furthermore, within the argument itself, as can be seen from the preceding response to the non-feminist version, proponents can be heard to deploy categorial arguments.

The dispute—the contestable character of the murders, of responses to them, and of commentaries on them—is, in its turn, subjected to explicit formulation of its consequences. But this is a matter for chapter 7, and we take it up there.

▼
CONCLUSION

It is tempting to conceive the materials we have considered in this chapter as evidence of a social contentiousness about the character of the problem signified by the Montreal Massacre. Further, such contentiousness might then be made to stand as evidence that various claims and counter claims were being made in both reportage and commentary about what the massacre was *as a social problem*. In other words, the sociologist might thereby be able to claim that our materials exhibited the claims and counterclaims provided for in the theory of the "social construction of social problems" (Spector and Kitsuse 1987; Loseke 1992, 1999; Holstein and Miller 1993; Miller and Holstein 1993; Best 1995; Sasson 1995). The dispute between feminist and non-feminist versions of the massacre might be rendered, for example, as a competition over "ownership" (Gusfield 1989) of the problem it represents. Our view is that whilst some may well understand and indeed use our materials in this way, for us there is no evidence *in the materials themselves* that either the parties to the dispute or the reporters of and commentators about it, in any way conceived of their own activities as constitutive of a sociologically defined social process. They may have argued about what the significance of the murders was, they may have disagreed about what collection to include the murders in, and the media may have played a disseminating role in relaying the various versions of what happened to their audiences. But to treat such activities as constitutive of the "social construction of a social problem" would be to confuse sociological theorizing with an appreciation of what the Montreal Massacre is as a members' phenomenon. Indeed, for members, as we have seen, it may have been a variety of things, but all bore down upon them with an overwhelming objectivity. If those members had been told that, when all is said and done, they were constructing a social problem, they would have looked at the teller in disbelief. Granted, if a kind of theoretical disruption of their natural attitude was wrested from them, they might have conceded that their beliefs were in fact constitutive of social reality, but such a product would have been one produced within the "construction of social problems language game" (Bogen and Lynch 1993).

As we said in chapter 1, we prefer not to get involved in these matters of sociological representation. Instead, we are inclined to transmit and make evident to our readers as far as is possible what the members who are our subjects of study are oriented to and how they are oriented to it. It seems to us that they were oriented to the Montreal Massacre in terms of its overwhelming objectivity and that they spoke of this in various categorially organized ways. It is our aim to describe this categorial order rather than subsume it under a sociological theory about what they were *really* up to.

PART 2

The Montreal Massacre and Moral Order

CHAPTER 6

Accounting for the Massacre: Categories and Social Structure

▼
INTRODUCTION

IN THIS CHAPTER OUR INTEREST is in members' methods of accounting for the murders. The attentive reader will have noticed that explanatory elements are already contained in various of the stories considered in the previous chapters. Such accounts occur in, and are thereby partly constitutive of, the crime story, the story about the killer, the killer's story, and notably the story of violence against women. Here our interest is in examining those accounts for their own formal features. In particular, our concern is with members' uses of social structure and social context as explanatory devices. A significant part of the Montreal Massacre as a members' phenomenon consists in the methods whereby it is produced, we might say "socialized," as a *societal* phenomenon. As we said in chapter 5, but did not analyze there, the transformation of the killings into a story of violence against women consisted not only in the collecting of the killer's actions with a range of other actions deemed instances of the phenomenon "violence against women" but also in their *explanation* in terms of "violence-against-women" theorizing, and in the *formulation of their consequences* for women and society generally. In this and the next chapter we will examine members' accounts of causes and consequences in our materials and take the opportunity to engage long-standing sociological debates about these matters.

We wish to show how membership categorization analysis, as ethnomethodology, can offer a novel point of view on traditional sociological problems by respecifying the study of such issues as the relation of individual and society, the link between social structure and social action, and the connection between motivation and action. It is our contention that all sociological areas as traditionally investigated, whether demarcated as theoretical or substantive, not only rest for their intelligibility on but also constitute forms of membership categorization on the part of the sociologist. Our style of presentation changes accordingly. In previous chapters our purpose was to exhibit *in* the news stories and commentary the use of various methods of practical reasoning through which they are put together. We attended closely to the materials and presented them in detail. Here and in the next chapter, in contrast, our tack is to more patiently develop a sociological position *on* some aspects of our materials. We write, then, more argumentatively and programmatically, and use the materials more illustratively. At the same time we seek to develop the account we have presented in outline elsewhere (Hester and Eglin 1997d, 1997e).

▼
SOCIOLOGY, ETHNOMETHODOLOGY, AND THE EXPLANATION OF CONDUCT

If sociology's original questions, such as "how is society possible?" and "how is social order possible?" were good ones, sociology's answers have been overwhelming in their partiality and spectacular in their omissions. The fundamental reason for this state of affairs and, in particular, for the lack of sociological attention to the detail of social life is sociology's preoccupation with *theorizing* its object of inquiry, rather than inspecting those naturally occurring sites of human activity in and through which social life is *done* and social order *accomplished* and *displayed*. In contrast, a key feature of ethnomethodology is its study policy, its analytic mentality, which insists on doing empirical studies, by working on materials to see what can be discovered in and from them, rather than selecting problems and data on the basis of some theoretically specified agenda (Sharrock and Watson 1989: 434–435; Hester and Eglin 1997b). From this point of view, sociologists have not only missed the detailed, interior "whatness" of social life, they have also unwittingly denied themselves access to the constituent practices through which social order is accomplished and members' sense of society manifested. This is not to deny sociology's achievements *on its own terms,* nor is it to adopt a constructionist model of society or social reality. The products of sociology's formal analytic (Garfinkel 1991) theorizing may be massive achievements in their own right, but they do not illuminate the endogenously accomplished orderliness of social activities and phenomena. Instead, they substitute externally generated theoretical models of how the social world works for an observationally based appreciation of how social life is ordered *from within.*

Ethnomethodology, from its inception, has sought to respecify sociological and criminological phenomena, to treat as a topic of inquiry in its own right that which is taken for granted as a resource in sociology, and to treat procedurally the social facts that are sociology's stock in trade. Studies (Garfinkel 1967; Cicourel 1964; etc) have shown that professional sociology relied upon and took for granted a panoply of everyday knowledge and practical reasoning, whose use rendered its subject matter intelligible and available in the first place. As Sharrock and Watson (1989: 433) declare, "Sociology itself is a natural language pursuit, one carried on and reported in some one of the variety of natural languages and one which requires, depends on and employs the (largely) unexamined descriptive resources of such language." In a similar vein Coulter (1974: 108) remarks,

> Sociologists generally share the natural-language of their subjects, and this has involved them in a tacit pre-understanding of their identification of the environment (social and physical) in linguistic categories. Ethnomethodology seeks to explore the dynamics of members' understandings as observable features of social settings, whilst holding that such dynamics also characterize the sociologists' procedures for recognizing data.

In this chapter, a particular variety of members' methods, namely members' methods of membership categorization, is considered with respect to a specific interactional task, namely the provision of accounts or explanations of conduct.

More recently and more particularly, we have shown (Hester and Eglin 1997d, 1997e) how professional sociology itself, as a socially organized activity, consists in a professional species of membership categorization analysis (MCA). MCA has tended to concentrate on personal membership categories to the exclusion of other kinds of categories, as in non-personal ones (but note Sacks's [1992a,b] work on "topic") and in particular "categories of social configuration" (Coulter 1982) or "collectivity categorizations" (Jayyusi 1984: 47, 52, etc.). In this chapter, our attention is focused not on sociologists as such, but on the deployment of a central sociological method, namely the use of social context in media discourse on the subject of the Montreal Massacre. That is, we examine how categories of social configuration are deployed in media accounts of the massacre. At the same time, in keeping with some of Sacks's early practice, we hope to learn something about professional sociologists' accounting practices by examining the equivalent practices in ordinary, lay-sociological use. A further exposition of our position can usefully begin with some remarks of Schegloff (1991).

▼

THE OPERATIONAL RELEVANCE OF SOCIAL CONTEXT

Of all sociology's concepts—race, class, gender, community, etc.—social context is perhaps most definitive of the sociological imagination or attitude. Under its auspices, sociologists are enjoined to place the local, situated, and personal in wider social frameworks, such as patriarchy, capitalism, and the global economy. To respecify context as *members' phenomena* is not to deny the importance of social context in the conduct of social life. Rather, it is to suggest that the issue of context is far more complicated and significant than is recognized in orthodox sociology (Hester and Eglin 1997b: 26–28). Thus, it is far too simplistic to presume the relevance of some sociological version of context as proposed by the sociologist on the assumption that "everybody knows" what *the* context for an action is. As Garfinkel (1967: 10) has put it, "not only does no concept of context-in-general exist, but every use of 'context' without exception is essentially indexical." The task, then, becomes conceived as one that treats context as a *members' phenomenon,* and that requires investigating how members take this into account in the course of their activities. Thus, in the view of Schegloff (1991: 49), one of the problems that is typically ignored in sociology is to show that a social context, or social structure, is *relevant* for those under investigation. Schegloff (1991: 48) rightly indicates that it is not enough to intuit that such structural features as power, gender, race, class, and so forth "have something to do with social action; rather, it has to be *demonstrated* and demonstrated *in detail,*" otherwise they remain analysts' intuitions at best. As Schegloff continues (1991: 51):

> If the sense of social structure we are dealing with is one that turns on the differential distribution of valued resources in society, whether status or power or money or any of the other "goods" whose distribution can be used to characterize social structure, then that implies a characterization or categorization of the participants on that occasion as one relevantly to be selected from that set of terms. But then the problem presents itself of the relevance of those terms to the participants for what they are doing. Without a show of that warrant, we are back to a "positivistic" stance, even though the animating concerns may be drawn from quite anti-positivistic theoretical sources or commitments.

And again:

> Now let us be clear about what is and what is *not* being said here. The point is not that persons are somehow *not* male or female, upper or lower class, with or without power, professors and / or students. They may be, on some occasion, demonstrably members of one or another of those categories. Nor is the issue that those aspects of the society do not matter, or did not matter on that occasion. We may share a lively sense that indeed they do matter, and that they mattered on that occasion, and mattered for just that aspect of some interaction on which we are focussing. There is still the problem of *showing from the details of the talk or other conduct in the materials* that we are analyzing that those aspects of the scene are what the parties are oriented to. *For that is to show the parties are embodying for one another the relevancies of the interaction and are thereby producing the social structure.*

It is clear that Schegloff's insistence on the *relevance* of structural/contextual categories for members is what distinguishes an ethnomethodological approach and an understanding that goes deeper than a theorist's surmise or imposition. Put simply, unlike conventional sociology, ethnomethodology does not *privilege* the relevance of particular versions of social contexts to what occurs in a setting. Rather, the relevance of versions of context is regarded as a members' phenomenon. This means the following: *that* a context is intelligible and available *as* a particular type of context is something provided for and oriented to by members; it is not to be presumed by authorial fiat. The issue is not whether it may be correct or incorrect to occasionally assert that members' talk occurs, for example, in capitalist society or in a context of patriarchal relations; what is important is the *operational relevance* of such contexts.[1]

Though not without its ambiguities, the discussion by Drew and Heritage (1992) of social structure and social context is instructive with regard to how context is deployable in ethnomethodological studies (see also Hester and Francis 2000). Thus, Drew and Heritage can be understood to reject what they describe as the "bucket theory" of context, in which interaction is viewed as "contained" within some pre-established social or institutional framework, and moulded by that framework to "fit with" its requirements, and in its place they propose an "analytic attitude" which they summarize as follows:

> utterances—and the social actions they embody—are treated as doubly contextual. First, utterances and actions are *context shaped.* Their contributions to an ongoing sequence of actions cannot be adequately understood except by reference to the context in which they participate. The term "context" is here used to refer to both the immediately local configuration of preceding activity in which an utterance occurs, and also the "larger" environment of activity within which that configuration is recognised to occur.... Second, utterances and actions are *context renewing.* Since every current utterance will form the immediate context of some next action in a sequence, it will inevitably contribute to the contextual framework in terms of which the next action will be understood. In this sense, the interactional context is continually being developed with each successive action. Moreover, each current action will, by the same token, function to renew (i.e., maintain, adjust or alter) any broader or more generally prevailing sense of context that is the object of the participants' orientations and actions (Drew and Heritage 1992: 18).

Thus, they offer two senses of context as something to which the parties to a local setting of interaction are oriented: (a) "the immediately local configuration of preceding activity in which an utterance occurs," and (b) "the 'larger' environment of activity within which that configuration is recognised to occur." The key phrase here is "recognised to occur." Insofar as this refers to members' recognitions and not to analysts' stipulations, then Drew and Heritage's remarks can serve as a useful point of ethnomethodological departure for the investigation of context as a members' phenomenon.[2] Furthermore, Drew and Heritage's second key point can be heard to allude to the reflexive relations between invocations of context and the constitution of those contexts. That is, any *use* of a context is itself a constituent feature of that context and thereby contributes to the sense of the context.

The view espoused by Schegloff (1991) and Drew and Heritage (1992) is also to be found in a rather more developed exposition by Coulter (1982), in Sharrock and Watson (1988), and in our own work (cited above). Before attending to the ways this plays itself out with reference to our data, some explication of these sources is in order.

▼
MEMBERSHIP CATEGORIZATION AND SOCIAL STRUCTURE

Whilst most of the work in MCA has been concerned with personal membership categories and categorization devices, the collectivity categorizations mentioned above provide a way of studying "social structures" ethnomethodologically, as Coulter (1982) indicates. That is, social structures or institutions are describable and analyzable in MCA terms. It allows us to see how members use categories of social configurations or collectivity-categorizations, such as the "stock exchange," the "army," the "military-industrial complex," the "school," the "aristocracy," the "middle class," the "state," "capitalist society," "them" and "us," as well as membership categorization devices like "family," "stage of life," etc. The uses to which such collectivity-categorizations may be put are as investigable as any other type of membership category or categorization device. Thus, social configurations may be used to provide the sense for a membership category, to impute a motive, contest an explanation, provide for the intelligibility of an action, and a whole host of other practical activities. The key point is that in MCA, as opposed to structuralist sociology, the uses of these collectivity-categorizations are respecified as topics of inquiry rather than as resources for sociological theorizing. Moreover, such a respecification sidesteps orthodox sociology's dichotomy between structural and interactional domains of social organization, a dichotomy that both provides such sociology with its characteristic topics and problems (including bridging the micro-macro divide) and establishes a basis for criticizing interpretive sociologists for leaving out the social structure (power, class, patriarchy, etc.). As Sharrock and Watson (1988) argue, social structure may be viewed as incarnate to social interaction. What we wish to add is that MCA affords a way of examining how social structures are articulated in the talking work of everyday life.

The ethnomethodological and, in particular, MCA conception of social structure discussed above allows us a particular vision of sociological practice and especially sociological practice of the structural variety. This we would suggest is a professionalized form of membership categorization. Thus, our interests are not limited to lay membership categorization, nor to the tacit membership categorization of professional substantive sociological work. Rather they extend to the work of professional members whose stock-in-trade is a distinctive collection of social configurations and membership categories, and where a major part of what is done with them is to examine the interconnections between categories of actions, categories of persons, and categories of social configurations. If, indeed, members' membership categorization analysis is folk sociology, then professional sociology is folk sociology writ large. MCA provides us with a method of seeing this in the detail of sociological inquiries. Though not expressed in the full-blown language of MCA we are using here, this direction of inquiry has to some extent been anticipated by Sharrock (1974: 45) in the following passage:

> Sociologists routinely treat the activities of society's members as being somehow related to one or another corpus of knowledge: it is supposed that there must be some connection between what members know and what they do. The use of such notions as "culture," "perspective," "ideology," and "world view" has not only been intended to convey the idea that members' activities are to be construed by reference to some corpus of knowledge but also that the corpus of knowledge itself must be viewed as being in some way associated with the collectivity in which the actors have membership. The problem for sociologists has not, then, been that of finding a relationship between any member's knowledge and his activities but, instead, that of interpreting the relationship between a collectivity's corpus of knowledge and the activities of its members.

This, we suggest, hints at the respecification of sociology's foundational methods as a topic of ethnomethodological inquiry. More directly related to our present programmatic remarks, Jayyusi (1984: 52) says, "Much of members' social theorising is organised through the production and provision for collectivities in talk as morally organised groups and the characterisation and description of individuals and their actions as relative to, and accountable in terms of, their membership in such groups." Moreover, she continues:

> Such work—of producing, displaying or invoking the morally organised character of collectivities, or the turning of collections of persons into collectivities—consists, then, of devices for *making sense of social structures*, of finding explanations for "social events," locating responsibility (in its widest context), predicting, ratifying accounts, clarifying domains of expectation, formulating courses of action and the like. (Jayyusi 1984: 52)

We can clearly do no more here than indicate in a preliminary way what we take to be the promise of this avenue of inquiry. We will develop brief illustrations for three standard sociological perspectives. The conceptual machinery comprising the various sociological perspectives and the uses to which they are put in sociological inquiry is a form of professional MCA. Thus the perspectives differ in terms of three major conceptual elements of MCA: (a) the models (membership category) both of the individual actor and collective actor

(collectivity-category) they employ, presuppose, or afford; (b) the membership categorization devices in which these actors are collected; and (c) the
features or predicates they attach to such theoretical categories of actor.

For a first example, in the *structural consensus perspective,* society is posited
as a system with constituent roles into which persons are socialized. These
ideas can be seen to be deployed according to the logic informing the use of categories, devices, and predicates. Categories are the roles, devices are the institutional collections of roles (such as comprise religion, family, education, work,
etc.), and predicates are role expectations. Much sociological practice under the
aegis of this perspective consists of the discovery and fabrication of sociological categories of persons whose assigned social characteristics (predicates),
derived from the social configurations within which they are sociologically
located, account for their behaviour.

Similarly, for a second example, we may note, after Jayyusi (52), a characteristic turn in *Marxist sociology* by which collections of persons are turned
into morally organized collectivities.

> The concept of "hegemonic" class, for instance, in the Marxist tradition is
> routinely made to work by constituting, through its situated use, a collec-
> tivity morally organised with respect to the ideas, values, commitments, etc.
> that are said to be hegemonic. It can also thus constitute another collec-
> tivity (the "hegemonised" one) as one that is morally organised in a sub-
> ordinate way, but which could be organised differently.

Finally, for a third example, in the *symbolic interactionist* tradition social action
is accounted for in terms of the cultural predicates (knowledge, belief, values,
norms, definitions of the situation, etc.) that are tied to particular collectivities
(for example, industrial workers, drug users, taxi drivers, cocktail waitresses).
It may be further understood as the outcome of category-bound strategic practices construed as deriving from, say, demand characteristics of the social configuration in which they are located. Thus the demands of the courtroom (say,
for disposing of cases) become the category-tied motives of such courtroom
personnel as public defender and thereby are made to account for, say, their
routine involvement in plea bargaining.

▼
SOCIAL STRUCTURE AND THE MONTREAL MASSACRE

We said in the previous chapter that in the commentaries following or accompanying the reporting of the murders the overarching story was that of male violence against women. That is, we said, the story in the commentaries was
fundamentally not only a crime story about the offender and his victims but
about what the murders represent. We examined there that aspect of this story's
telling that comprised showing or finding the *collection* to which the killings
belonged—that is, what kind of killing it was. As we saw, this became a con-

tested matter, a matter of dispute. And, as we said above, here and in the next chapter we want to examine the story insofar as it comprises, respectively, explaining or accounting for the occurrence of the killings, and formulating the consequences of them. Our approach to *our* analysis of members' explanations of the murders is to see them in terms of *members' own* category analysis. One class of such analyses involves members' use of *personal* membership categories whilst others deploy categories of *social configuration.* As we shall see, these are frequently used in combination, as commentators seek to accommodate both the desire to locate causal or moral responsibility in the actor himself, and the urge to locate causes in the wider society. We shall consider each class in turn, using the analysis to exhibit the approach to the understanding of social context and social structure outlined above.

One variety of the use of personal membership categories in explaining the murders involves the gender-category of the victims. This is most graphically rendered in the following excerpt:

E111   FOURTEEN WOMEN are dead for one reason: they are women. Their male classmates are still alive for one reason: they are men. (Dec 8 [5])

This account implies Lépine's own category analysis, his deliberate selection of his victims because they are women, and more specifically in his eyes, feminists. As we noted in chapter 4, citing Watson, providing a category to characterize the victims of murder can suffice to convey the killer's motive for killing them.

A second variety of the explanatory use of personal membership categories involves the imputation of predicates to the category incumbent such that the act in question follows from his or her category membership. Some commentaries make use of the membership category "lunatic" (or "madman" or "insane person" or "crazed man"). For example:

E112   ...But Yvan Asselin, president of the Quebec Order of Engineers, said there is no reason for female engineers to feel targeted by the massacre. Instead, he suggested, the profession itself has been the victim of an unfair attack by feminists.

"It's sad that it happened," Mr. Asselin said. "But it is not because women are unwelcome in the profession that a crazed man attacked those women." (Dec 12 [4])

The use of "crazed man" here may be said to be designed to counter the feminist analysis its user opposes. "Crazed man" invokes the predicate craziness (or mental illness) that is sufficient both to account for the murders and to discount other, rationalist explanations. This "excusing" practice is itself named and countered in the feminist response that the "appeal to mental illness is a familiar excuse" (Dec 12 [2]), and that it "would be a great mistake, I think, to see this incident as some kind of freak accident, the act of a madman that has nothing to do with the society in which we live" (Dec 8 [5]). Again, there is irony in these commentators' (presumably unwitting) replication of Lépine's own analysis of his actions in the suicide letter, including the anticipation that others would designate him a "Mad Killer." What Lépine, the anti-feminist, foresaw as the danger of the insanity ascription, namely that it removes the agency from the would-be rational actor's acts and substitutes for them symptoms of the disease he is suffering from, can become a tool in the kit of the feminist commentator.

Other commentaries make use of the membership category "men," attributing violence against women to incumbents of this category. The use of "men" in this way is evident in the following extract:

E113   At that gathering, men were blamed for the massacre in a letter which circulated among 56 women at the candlelight vigil organized by the Northern Women's Centre.

"This is a men's issue, this is men's violence; this terrorism and these deaths are your creations and your shame," Sasha McInnes wrote in an open letter to men. (Dec 11 [4])

Some commentaries make use of category-predicate combinations in transformations of "men" in "anti-women" and "anti-feminist" ways. Thus, for example:

E114   But someone we know is assaulting women: a colleague, a close friend, a casual acquaintance. In a discussion paper entitled The Politics of Women Abuse, author Melanie Randall speaks of "a national epidemic"—between 2.5 million and 6.25 million Canadian women are assaulted by the men with whom they are involved.

Behind every epidemic is a cause. These assaults are committed by men of all ages, from all backgrounds. Men in stained overalls and three-piece suits, high-school dropouts and tenured professors.

We see women pursuing careers once considered male bastions and we feel wronged. We see their growing financial independence and we feel threatened. We see women's bodies as ours to violate. We don't understand their bodies. What we don't understand or can't control frustrates us, and frustration is a good enough excuse for aggression. (Dec 8 [4])

The writer collects himself and other men into the course-of-action type "men," a category to which he ascribes certain predicates as effects of causes residing in transformations in the status of women. Thus men "feel wronged," "feel threatened," "see women's bodies as ours to violate," "don't understand [women's] bodies," become "frustrate[d]," turn to "aggression." Similarly, in the following extract the predicate that is combined with "many men" is "deep-seated fear and resentment," which results in a violent "rearguard action" against women:

E115   If the arrogance of male dominance is to be found, naked and unashamed, at the heart of our democratic system and in centres of higher learning, it is evident that a *deep-seated fear and resentment* is at work among many men in the larger society. The passing of the old order, just and reasonable as the changes are, has proved indigestible to some, and they have chosen to launch their own forms of *rearguard action*—raging perhaps at the "Ms" designation which removes marital status as a major identifier of womankind in print, or deploring the erosion of the traditional family in which mother does not own a briefcase. (Dec 8 [3]; emphasis added)

It is worth noting how these two extracts may be heard as making more or less the same case, though the first uses the apparently global term "men," while the second qualifies "men" with "many." As Sacks (1992a; 1975) says in "Everyone Has to Lie" with respect to the use of the term "everyone," in standard uses such a category does not literally mean "all the people in the world." Rather, it is categorially limited to a particular, if unspecified, collection of persons. In the descriptions under consideration here, "men" also is recognizably limited categorially, namely to those who are chauvinist or anti-feminist and as such, men for whom "feeling threatened" and "aggression" are category predicates. As Sacks (1992a: 550–551) puts it:

Now, "everyone" might seem in the first place to be a "summative" term. But let's leave it open as a possibility that it's a "categorial" term, and governed in the way those are. It might be, for example, that terms like "everyone" and "no one" stand in juxtaposition to one another. If you come home from a party, for example, and someone asks you who was there and you say, "No one," then, that there were 12 people there doesn't matter for the correctness of "no one." "No one" means "under some formulation of who should have been there, no one was there." Likewise, it might be the case that when asked, "Who was there?" somebody says "Everyone," then there are formulations of "everyone" which provide for the fact that "everyone was there" indeed, though millions of people weren't.

One way in which "defendants" standardly seek to defeat an accusatory argument such as that developed in the extracts above is to *treat* the term "men" as summative rather than categorial, and then to assert that the argument does not hold in 100 percent of cases. It was perhaps from a desire to forestall such counter-arguments that the author of E115 preferred the qualified expression "many men."

Sociological categorial accounts stress the wider categories of social configuration in terms of which male violence against women in general and these murders in particular are understandable. For example, having invoked "the larger society" and "the old order," the author of E115 continues:

E116   It would be rash to build too elaborate a structure of cause and effect on the fragile base of one demented mind, but the horrifying executions at the University of Montreal do emerge from a *social context* and cannot be disowned. (Dec 8 [3]; emphasis added)

This editorial opinion is matched on the same day in an op-ed we have already quoted above:

E117   It would be a great mistake, I think, to see this incident as some kind of freak accident, the act of a madman that has nothing to do with the *society* in which we live. The killer was angry at women, at feminism, at his own loss of power. He yelled: "You're all a bunch of feminists" on his way to killing 14 women. (Dec 8 [5]; emphasis added)

Elsewhere an anthropologist is quoted as follows:

E118   "I think we have to understand how virulent and malevolent sexist feelings can be," he said in a telephone interview. "Whenever a social group rejects its subservience, as women everywhere have been doing, it threatens those in power…[*sic*] No catastrophe is unrelated to major changes in *society*." (Dec 11 [4]; emphasis added)

As is evident in E116 and E117, personal and sociological category analyses are here being combined. Other examples of this combining follow:

E119   "The event did not happen in a vacuum," said Ms Nero, a spokesman for the Committee de Defence des Femmes…
    "It was a *lunatic* who went on a rampage with the reinforcement of a lot of *misogynist social values* and a message that violence against women is okay," she said. (Dec 8 [2]; emphasis added)

E120   "People are recognizing that it's the work of a *madman* who has been fed by *social attitudes* on the gender issue," said Rev. Dorothy Barker, chaplain for the University of Guelph's ecumenical campus ministry, in an interview after the ceremony. (*KWR*, Dec 9 [1]; emphasis added)

E121   *Crazed* as he may well have been, the killer who carefully separates males from females before the shooting began absorbed his attitudes from the society around him. Collectively, unconsciously and sometimes overtly, we have provided him with all the *context* (albeit wildly distorted) he needed.

> This is a *society* that still moves with reluctance, and sometimes with bitter resistance, toward acceptance of the idea that women are entitled to equality in areas formerly dominated by men. Despite the changes that have been made—or possibly because of them— there is fertile ground for the misogynist or male chauvinist.
> ...
> It would be rash to build too elaborate a structure of cause and effect on the fragile base of one *demented mind,* but the horrifying executions at the University of Montreal do emerge from a *social context* and cannot be disowned.[3] (Dec 8 [3]; emphasis added)

We note (a) that the authors of these extracts invoke the category of social context as an account of the murders ("The event did not happen in a vacuum" [E119], "a madman who has been fed by social attitudes" [E120], the murders "emerge from a social context" [E121]); (b) that the authors characterize the context in terms of *normative values* ("misogynist social values and a message that violence against women is okay" [E119], "the idea that women are entitled to equality" [E121]) and *social attitudes* ("social attitudes on the gender issue" [E120]), and (c) that violence against women (and in particular the Montreal Massacre) is therefore to be seen as an example of conformity to anti-female values and attitudes. This is a structural-functionalist kind of account. But if it is true to say that the appeal to social context in these extracts exhibits a structural-functionalist form of reasoning, that must be immediately qualified by pointing out that the kind of functionalism involved is of the "conflict" sort.

That is, social context is formulated in a particular way. It is formulated in terms remarkably similar to those that are known as the feminist variety of "structural conflict theory" within sociology. This perspective has sometimes been called the "feminist-conflict" position (Kleck and Sayles 1990; Hester and Eglin 1992: 20). Thus, in particular, one author offers a model of the social structure of male-female relations consisting of two positions, superordinate/ subordinate; the model is thus categorially ordered; it provides for a moral order of relations and activities; it prevails at Time One, but is challenged by the subordinates at Time Two; adherents to the model object; they are angry at those who challenge the categorial/moral order; it is these changes that are connected to the massacre. Moreover, we note that Lépine is portrayed as a party to such conflict; he speaks, acts, and analyzes as an incumbent of one category belonging to the device "parties to male/female conflict" or "parties to patriarchal relations."

Other commentators sought to spread the causal net (and the collection to which the murders belonged) far wider. Michael Valpy's three columns in the *Globe and Mail* are notable in this regard. He might be said to make the case for the "mass murder" interpretation of Lépine's actions. In the first column,

"Systematic slaughter is without precedent" (Dec 8 [6]), he subsumes the killings under the category "mass murders," adduces a criminologist to describe and explain the social distribution of the phenomenon, classifies the phenomenon by type of victim ("blacks, Asians, Hispanics, children, and workmates"), then invites expert commentary on what is now the novel type, the mass murder of women:

E122   Before the mid-1960s, mass murders were very few. Criminologist James Fox of Boston's Northeastern University says there now are 30 a year in the United States—murders which he classifies as having more than four victims. He predicts a steady increase, as more and more baby-boomers become discontent with life.

   He said seven of the 10 biggest mass murders in US history have occurred in the 1980s. He talked about the contributing criteria of job dissatisfaction, too few social supports such as close friends and family, the greater incidence of media-portrayed violence and the greater availability of high-powered weapons.

   Mass murderers have chosen blacks, Asians, Hispanics, children and workmates as their targets. But we haven't had this happen before: the choice of women.

   Senator Lorna Marsden, a University of Toronto sociologist specializing in women's issues, characterized the Montreal murders as the historical continuity of violence against women. (Dec 8 [6])

In the second column, "Litany of social ills created Marc Lepine" (Dec 11 [3]; see figure 1), he argues the case that attributing the killings to the collection of, and thereby explaining them in terms of, "men's abuse of women…lets too many people off the hook."

FIGURE 1

Litany of social ills created Marc Lepine
Michael Valpy

Marc Lepine's killing of 14 women is being turned solely into an issue of men's abuse of women. This lets too many people off the hook.

   To be sure, I have asked questions of my 16-year-old daughter I have never asked before. Has she ever felt physically threatened by males? Yes. Has she ever felt physically afraid of males? Yes. This is my precious daughter, in her normal, secure, middle-class world.

   "It was so close to us. He could have come into our school, he could have come after us women." Us Women is what she said.

   But what if Marc Lepine had gone after blacks, Asians, children as the cause of his woes, as other mass murderers have gone after blacks, Asians, children? And what if my daughter were black, Asian, a child?

In the past two decades, mass murder has become a footprint of North America.

Marc Lepine fit to a T the mass murderer's profile. The loner, pathologically alienated from the supports of close friends and family. The person imbued with the sense of powerlessness over his own life in a world of larger and larger impersonal institutions. The devotee of Rambo cultural imagery, seeing in it the solution to the individual's societal impotence.

Will we go demonstrating in the streets this week—holding vigils, carrying candles, wearing white scarves—in protest against the depersonalization of humanity in a First World society greed-driven to constructing corporate and social structures that screw the poor and robotize the rest of us?

Will we demand that our politicians take action against spirit-breaking housing costs, against the shattering humility of private charity food banks, against the untrammelled growth dehumanizing our cities and destroying the soul-nurturing tranquility of the rural landscape, against the obscenity of $300 teddy bears in Christmas toyshops.

Will we boycott the products of corporations that treat their workers as faceless cogs, mere human machinery to be dismantled at whim, tossed out, say, if there is a chance for a few extra bucks profit by moving the factory south of the border?

Will we denounce the Prime Minister's unctuous hypocrisy? "Why such violence in a society that considers itself civilized and compassionate?" Brian Mulroney asked.

The answer, in part, is because his government reduces unemployment insurance benefits and expenditures on health, education and welfare while his Finance Minister shills $1,000 bottles of cognac in a Toronto magazine.

Mr. Mulroney's government is a statement—such as we haven't heard in Canada in this century—of our evaporating social compassion. In the five years of his administration, one million Canadians—40 per cent of them children—have become dependent upon private charity food banks in order to eat.

Can there be a woman—or man—in Canada who does not recognize the breeding grounds for Marc Lepines? The stone weights of poverty and powerlessness on families. The urban isolation. The depersonalized workplace. The ghastly cultural images of resolution ... get your gun, get your military fatigues, be a man, take a man's way out ...

Can someone—maybe Justice Minister Douglas Lewis—explain why anyone needs to buy automatic or semi-automatic weapons? We've shot up just about all the animals within easy reach. What's left ... except blacks, Asians, children, women?

It is the social conditions that produce Marc Lepine—and more and more Marc Lepines—that concern me. Not enough of us have been driven mad yet for us to be really interested in building a civilized, compassionate society.

Source: *Globe and Mail*, Monday, December 11, 1989, A8.

Rather than being (merely) a case of a mass killing of *women* and hence an instance of *male violence against women*, Valpy argues again that the killings belong to the collection "mass murder" and that along with other mass murders (for example of blacks, Asians, etc.) the murder of the Montreal women has to be seen in terms of a wider social configuration: "a world of larger and larger impersonal institutions." In a kind of sociological functionalist analysis the author lists social ills that are apparently connected to mass murder: "the depersonalization of humanity in a First World society greed-driven to constructing corporate and social structures that screw the poor and robotize the rest of us"; "spirit-breaking housing costs," "the shattering humility of private charity banks," "the untrammelled growth dehumanizing our cities and destroying the soul-nurturing tranquility of the rural landscape," the treatment of "workers as faceless cogs, mere human machinery to be dismantled at whim, tossed out, say, if there is a chance for a few extra bucks profit." And more particularly, because "government reduces unemployment insurance benefits and expenditures on health, education and welfare," and because of a wider "evaporating social compassion," we have "the breeding grounds for Marc Lepines. The stone weights of poverty and powerlessness on families. The urban isolation. The depersonalized workplace. The ghastly cultural images of resolution...get your gun, get your military fatigues, be a man, take a man's way out." The passage is, in its way, a remarkable theorization of the relations between social structural conditions, culture and government policy. In short, "It is the social conditions that produce Marc Lepine—and more and more Marc Lepines—that concern me. Not enough of us have been driven mad yet for us to be really interested in building a civilized, compassionate society."

We note here that not only are wider contextual features in the form of various categories of social configuration being invoked but also that there is more to the commentary than cause-and-effect analysis. The commentator can be clearly heard to allocate blame for the events. Indeed, this blame allocation was hinted at earlier in the *Globe and Mail* (Dec 8 [3]) editorial writer's account ("cannot be disowned"). In allocating blame to the "wider society" and by implication to "us," the author can be heard to engage in moral ordering work. Thus, by extension, the *offenders* in this case include those responsible for the objectionable social configurations and not just the murderer who emerged from them. There is also a hint of excuse in this account, namely that Lépine was "driven mad" by the social context in which he was "socialized."

Such theorizing affords clues, perhaps, to the hidden normative character of professional functionalist-sociological theorizing.

In the third column, "Risk of murder linked to non-domestic roles" (Dec 12 [6]), Valpy again gives a voice to social scientists, this time to test the thesis that there is a "growing 'male backlash against feminism'" that may explain Lépine's actions. This most professionally sociological of the three articles evokes (but does not mention) Durkheim's concept of anomy, or insufficient regulation, as an explanation of women's increased risk of being murdered. It is perhaps worth providing Durkheim's account here to appreciate the long explanatory tradition in which Valpy's column stands. By anomy, Durkheim meant that "loss of place" or the experience of "not knowing one's place" that comes from sudden changes of fortune. One's sense of social status, of where one belongs, of what one may reasonably aspire to—these matters are largely given by one's occupational rank in society. But it is just the character of industrial, as opposed to feudal, society to be struck with periodic crises, the effect of which is to upset the balance of things. Whether the crisis is one of boom or bust, the old scale is upset: "something like a declassification occurs," Durkheim says in *Suicide*. Since no "living being can be happy or even exist unless his needs are sufficiently proportioned to his means," and since in humans that regulation is not physically built in, it must be moral in origin. But since society is the source of moral regimens then social change brings moral deregulation. "Appetites, not being controlled by a public opinion become disoriented, no longer recognize the limits proper to them." This state of societal dis-ease eventuates in a rise in suicide rate. In this way Durkheim explains the rise in suicide rate at times of economic boom or bust. Moreover, in the industrial and commercial occupational groups "the state of crisis and anomy is constant and, so to speak, normal"—thus the higher suicide rates of these groups.

However, for periods of economic depression the aggregate rise in suicide rates conceals variation by class: suicide rates rise in the upper classes but do not change significantly among the lower classes. Instead, *homicide* rates increase in the lower classes. In their *Suicide and Homicide*, Henry and Short (1954) introduced a "frustration-aggression" hypothesis into a basically Durkheimian theory to explain this. Economic loss was said to cause frustration which was said to cause acts of aggression. *The powerless directed their aggression at others whom they held responsible for their losses, whereas the powerful directed it at themselves.* Thus, when times were bad, lower-class individuals committed more homicides, upper-class individuals more suicides (see Eglin 1985). Valpy's column draws on current sociological research in which moral deregulation resulting from *gender declassification* is the pertinent phenomenon. The "more women step outside traditional domestic roles" the greater the rate of "excess female homicide" (presumably above a Durkheimian equilibrium figure for "normal" female homicide) consequent upon women losing the "protective advantage [Durkheim again] against murder [from] remain[ing] in traditional settings."

▼
CONCLUSION

PROFESSIONAL SOCIOLOGISTS do not have privileged access to ideas of social context. Lay persons make use of such a method for making sense and for providing accounts.[4] Such explanatory uses of social context by laypeople are similar to the methods of professional sociologists. Are professional sociological accounts parasitic on lay members' methods? Are they just extensions thereof? Such accounts do moral ordering work, allocating blame and responsibility. Not for nothing, then, is sociology a moral science. Social configurations have predicates in the same way as personal membership categories do; that is, actions follow from (are conceptually tied to) particular social configurations. Furthermore, we note that such moral ordering work is in line with the anthropomorphization of social configurations and the increasingly prevalent combination of critical with descriptive ethnography.

CHAPTER 7

The Functions of the Massacre: Categories and Consequences

▼
INTRODUCTION

OUR INTEREST IN THIS CHAPTER is with the media formulations of the consequences of the Montreal Massacre. Our materials permit us to respecify as a members' phenomenon a traditional topic in the sociology of crime and deviance, namely their functions for society as a whole or for particular parts of society. That is, a further readily observable feature of the *Montreal Massacre* was its functional character, *for members*. We stress functionality as a members' phenomenon to mark the difference between functionalist theorizing as found in professional sociology and its appearance and use in members' talk and action. Thus, much of the reportage and commentary on the massacre exhibited a discernible functionalist orientation: the massacre was not only regrettable, condemnable, accountable, and so forth, it not only occasioned searching for an explanation (recall chapter 6), it was also analyzed as having certain consequences or functions for sections of and sometimes all of society. Before documenting this, and exploring some of its organizational features, a brief detour to lay out the key difference between mainstream sociological functionalism and an ethnomethodological attitude towards such matters will be taken.

▼
SOCIOLOGY, ETHNOMETHODOLOGY, AND THE FUNCTIONS OF CRIME AND DEVIANCE

Since at least Durkheim's famous third chapter in *The Rules of Sociological Method* (1982 [1895]) on rules for distinguishing the normal and the pathological, the argument that crime (deviance) is functional has become a standard feature of sociological theorizing of the functionalist kind. Durkheim argued that crime is not only normal for a given type of society at a given stage of its development, but that it is also necessary (Sharrock 1984). It serves to provide society with recurrent opportunities both to maintain indispensable moral boundaries and to adapt them to changing environmental circumstances. It is clearly the *response* to crime that is critical to Durkheim's theorizing here. It is the opportunity to *criminalize* action and actor that is the crucial element. This theoretical step allows those approaches to crime and deviance for which criminalization is the central phenomenon to find Durkheim's argument congenial to their point of view. Thus it is that interactionist and constructionist textbooks in the sociology of crime and deviance commonly include Durkheim's argument (for example, Box 1981 [1971]; Grusky and Pollner 1981; Hester and Eglin 1992).[1]

The functionalist argument depends on the acts of *denouncing* the crime and the criminal being made visible to the population so that they may have their unintendedly integrative effects. The prevailing media of communication in the society then become the necessary vehicles for re-presenting the criminalizing acts carried out in courtrooms and other such criminalizing settings. That crime stories, it is often said, seem to occupy such a prominent part of media content is then readily explained in term of this theory. What is less attended to is just how any particular crime report (or a series of them) accomplishes such a functional outcome.

Now it is true, at least since Spector and Kitsuse (1987 [1977]), that investigators have attended to the claims-making activities of moral (Becker 1963), professional (Hagan and Leon 1977) and program (Johnson 1981) entrepreneurs for the ways in which putatively troublesome conditions come to be constructed as "social problems" such as "violent crime" or "violence against women" (e.g., Pfohl 1977; Gusfield 1981; Tierney 1982; Loseke 1992; Leyton 1992; Jenkins 1994, etc.). And interactionist studies have long attended to the organizational and interactional features of deviance attribution and processing by social control agents such as the police and court personnel through which particular actions and actors are assigned some deviant status or label (Rubington and Weinberg 1987). In both constructionist and interactionist traditions this has included fairly close attention being given to the organizational and rhetorical features of media reporting of such conditions (for example, Fishman 1980; Best 1995; McCormick 1995; Potter and Kappeler 1998; Ferrell and Websdale 1999, etc.).

Understood as a form of micro-sociology, ethnomethodological studies might be thought to play some kind of remedial role in the illumination of the topics of the substantive sociological inquiry. Such an understanding exhibits what may be called an *incorporationist* or *social constructionist* view of ethnomethodology. From this point of view, ethnomethodological studies are regarded as providing the minutiae overlooked by other forms of sociological inquiry into the social processes involved in, for example, the social construction of deviance. Where sociologists have tended to produce decontextualized accounts of social action, ethnomethodology can supplement these crude depictions of social life by its close attention to the in situ specifics of social interaction. Both sociologists and ethnomethodologists look through the same lens, so the difference between them is simply one of the sharpness of focus. Because of this continuity of vision, ethnomethodological studies can be *incorporated* into the sociological mainstream. For us, such a conception elides a key difference between sociological and ethnomethodological accounts. Thus, in this incorporationist conception what the members of society do and say are viewed as constitutive of *sociologically defined* events and processes, including the construction of social problems, the exercise of power, the social constitution of gender, race relations, the manufacture of crime, social class, and the social construction of deviance. This approach conceives of social action, including language use, as a resource for the solution of sociological problems. Thus, in relation to the functions of deviance, the media are cast into a role in a sociological drama rather than being approached as a site of locally ordered social action in its own right. As we indicated in chapter 1, the incorporation of ethnomethodology into sociological theories of crime and deviance contradicts ethnomethodology's indifference to the theoretical preoccupations of sociology. Thus, while for sociology the nature and functions of deviance are matters of theoretical debate, for ethnomethodology they are not issues about which any *theoretical stance* needs to be or should be taken (Hester and Francis 1997). Rather, ethnomethodology seeks to examine the ways in which concerns with deviance inform members' locally ordered practical action and practical reasoning. In contrast to sociological theorizing, its concern is to describe the mundane practices in and through which persons are oriented to issues of what is deviant and what its significance may be in the course of such activities as reporting, describing, questioning, interpreting, deciding, explaining, and formulating deviance. Accordingly, the problem is not to theorize the functions of deviance; rather, it is to examine what deviance is *for members*, and to do so by inspecting how that is made available in the detail of social interaction. In this book we have been concerned with examining how deviance is described, explained, understood, and formulated, in short *ordered*, in a specific context, namely media coverage of the Montreal Massacre. This permits the respecification of the *functions* of deviance because an integral feature of media coverage of the Montreal Massacre concerned the question of its significance for society.

▼
RESPECIFYING THE FUNCTIONS OF CRIME AS MEMBERS' PHENOMENA

There has been a marked aversion in sociological circles to functionalism over the last thirty years or so. In part this was due to the apparently consensual and conservative character of its theorizing. It was thus pointed out that the consequences identified as functional for society were functional for society as a whole. This clearly neglected how functions were skewed in favour of particular sections of society. Furthermore, in terms of the various versions of conflict theory, such skewing was, it was argued, inevitably in favour of those with most to gain from prevailing social arrangements. The aversion was also due partly to the fact that functionalists approached their phenomena in terms of a systems perspective. Parsons, for example, asked what requirements social action would have to have in order for it to fit with the needs of the social system. Against this, the entire action frame of reference (encompassing symbolic interactionism and phenomenology) emphasized attending to social action from the point of view of the social actor.

These problems with functionalism, we suggest, do not mean that we have to reject it altogether as an idea. It is patently obvious that social action is routinely, not to say unavoidably, consequential. The ethnomethodological turn requires, however, that we examine in what ways members themselves analyze such events as the Montreal Massacre as consequential. The functions of crime and deviance are here respecified, then, not as phenomena to which the sociologist has special access, but as members' phenomena. Indeed, we would suggest that sociologists' particular claims in this regard are fundamentally no different from ordinary members' everyday methods of formulating the significance, and the consequences (both intended and unintended), of crime and deviance. Of course, we do not single out sociological functionalism as unique in this respect since it is plain that all varieties of sociology offer specialized and professionalized versions of practices widely deployed in everyday life, as we argued in chapter 6. Sociological functionalism makes a distinction between manifest and latent functions. Either way, these are consequences of the act or event in question. As such, sociological accounts trade off a common, everyday practice, namely formulating the consequences of acts and events. How then did members formulate the functions of the Montreal Massacre?

▼

MEMBERS' FORMULATIONS OF THE FUNCTIONS OF THE MASSACRE

In the articles that comprise our corpus of data, members are reported formulating in so many words the functions or consequences that the massacre was being seen to have. Here is a summary list, with abbreviated quotation of their sources in the media accounts.

realize / realization

E123   "It made us *realize* how vulnerable we are, particularly for those of us who had been quite heavily involved in the panty-raid issue, because that debate got quite verbally violent and aggressive, and this threw us back to that time," said Sharon Severinski, a graduate student in social work. (*KWR*, Dec 13 [1]; emphasis added)

E124 When these incidents happen "we *realize* that as women, we live in bondage in the common fear that we have," Coulter said. "All of us have experienced this very personally." (*KWR*, Dec 11 [4]; emphasis added)

E125 Two women staying at Anselma House, K-W's shelter for battered women and children, were both hit with a *sickening realization* as they watched the lead story on television recently.

"That could have been my husband doing that to me." (*KWR*, Dec 18; emphasis added)

reminded / reminder

E126 Now there is little that is comforting to say to women. It is a time for grief for all of us; grief for those who have died, and pain at being *reminded* of how deep misogyny still runs in our society. (Dec 8 [5]; emphasis added)

E127 That was the message that many women have received from the massacre—a *reminder* of the violence that women face every day, the crowd was told. (*KWR*, Dec 11 [4]; emphasis added)

affirms / acutely aware / brought out / feel / implications / echoed / rang true

E128 "Residents in the shelter are very upset," Spies said. "It *affirms* that many of their spouses could have, and still could, kill them."

Former residents have called, some asking about self-defence courses, she said. "It's really *brought out* how vulnerable and fearful they still are."

Staff now *feel* the fear too, along with residents, said Sue Coulter, public education and volunteer co-ordinator at Anselma House. "They are us," Coulter said.

...

But suddenly, and horribly, women have all become *acutely aware* of their fear, Coulter said.

And that's a point, too often missed, in the debate over the *implications* of Lepine's attack on women at the Montreal campus, said Paula Caplan, a Toronto psychologist and one of Canada's leading feminists.

The point, she said, is that Lepine's rampage with a semi-automatic rifle "*echoed*" the experiences of many women in Canada.

"It *rang true* for many, many women. That's what matters. That's what needs to be recognized. It felt like a shock, but not a surprise." (*KWR*, Dec 18; emphasis added)

symbolic / symbol / demonstrates

E129   Heald [Susan Heald, a sociology professor of Wilfrid Laurier University], vigil organizer Anna Toth, and local activist Sue Coulter said the killing of the engineering students was *symbolic* of the continuing violence against women. (*KWR,* Dec 11 [4]; emphasis added)

E89   Melody McLoughlin Marratto, a chaplain at St. Jerome's College, told the crowd that "for the incest survivor, the battered women, the rape victim, what happened in Montreal can only be understood as a *symbol* of the larger problem of men's violence against them." (*KWR,* Dec 14; emphasis added)

E130   Elliot Leyton, an anthropologist at Memorial University in Newfoundland, said the killings *demonstrate* how male chauvinism threatens women's lives. (Dec 11 [4]; emphasis added)

raises concerns / puts…in a very different light / raises questions

E131   Pierre Belanger, dean of engineering at McGill University, said the killings nonetheless *raise concerns* about the profession's image.
        Sexist publications put out by engineering students at many universities across the country may no longer be acceptable in this new environment, he noted, adding that "the massacre *puts them in a very different light.*" (Dec 12 [4]; emphasis added)

E132   After the meeting, Mr Mulroney told reporters: "This man singled out women in a completely criminal and insensitive fashion. It's an isolated incident, but it *raises questions* about violence in our society and about violence against women." (Dec 8 [2]; emphasis added)

put…back on centre stage

E133   Although the speeches steered clear of the panty-raid issue which had earlier rocked the university, people interviewed after the service said the shooting has *put the whole debate about male attitudes toward women back on centre stage* at WLU. (*KWR,* Dec 13 [1]; emphasis added)

is a grievous blow

E134   A Canadian expert on mass murderers says the slayings of 14 women at the University of Montreal last week is "*a grievous blow*" to relations between men and women. (Dec 11 [4]; emphasis added)

relegated...to the back pages

E135 "Yes, we have *relegated the Sunshine Girl to the back pages,* in light of the enormity of the tragedy and the nature of it," said Sun associate editor Lorrie Goldstein. (*KWR*, Dec 13 [2]; emphasis added)

more awareness / looking at the roles ... more carefully

E136 "As far as news content goes, we haven't changed anything," Morris said. "*I think there's a lot more awareness out there now among the male reporters of the feminist case in this terrible shooting...[sic].*

"They're *looking at the roles of men and women much more carefully,*" he said. "But there have been no policy directives at all." (*KWR*, Dec 13 [2]; emphasis added)

had an impact / consciousness raised / shocked ... into reality / action

E137 The shooting has *had an impact* on some men, especially those who were already trying to improve gender relationships, [Severinski] said. (*KWR*, Dec 13 [1]; emphasis added)

E138 The tragedy, so devastating to women who feel vulnerable to violence from men, has also *had an impact* on some K-W men searching for answers to what is being seen as a "male issue."

...

Caplan said growing numbers of men have abruptly had their *consciousness raised* in the wake of the massacre.

...

Caplan said the Montreal massacre has had a stunning impact on men.

"The majority of men I have heard, and heard about, are saying this has *shocked them into reality,* over sexual jokes, over their failure to support equal pay legislation, over women's rights to reproductive freedom, and adequate day care."

"It has *shocked them into action,*" Caplan said. (*KWR*, Dec 18; emphasis added)

relate it to other struggles

E139 [Heald] said women can see in the massacre their own personal experience with male violence and can *relate it to other struggles*

in our society—blacks, homosexuals, jews [sic] and communists.
(*KWR*, Dec 11 [4], emphasis added)

We want to bring out three features of these members' formulations of functions. First, the consequences they articulate or express are, at the same time, quite various, quite particular and, for many of them, quite general in character. Second, an unavoidable feature of their variety and particularity is the categorizations they afford of the parties (persons, groups, organizations, constituencies…) for whom the massacre is said to have these consequences or functions. Third, there is the noticeably unremarkable collection of identities of those who come to be selected by media personnel to formulate and express the massacre's consequences for those constituencies.

▼
THE VARIETY, PARTICULARITY, AND GENERALITY OF MEMBERS' FUNCTIONALIST FORMULATIONS

The variety of functions that persons interviewed in these news stories ascribe to the massacre is already at least partially indicated by the eleven-part list we have drawn up above. While constructed in the first place for the convenience of presenting the items this way for the reader's scrutiny, the list also both collects similar instances together and separates those that are different, in rough groupings. Our purpose is not to give a comprehensive, detailed, and precise linguistic account of the semantic and pragmatic similarities and differences of the emphasized expressions and their uses. Rather, our point is simply to bring out the *variety* contained in the list. If the list's length is a first indication of that variety a second indication is afforded by the following paraphrase of it:

> The massacre is described as making women realize their vulnerability to men's violence, and their common bondage in fear of violent men. It affirms, brings out, and makes them be aware of and feel that vulnerability and fear. It is a symbol and reminder of men's violence against women, and raises questions about it. It rang true for many women, echoing their experience. It is a reminder and demonstration of deep societal misogyny and the mortal threat to women of male chauvinism. It puts the debate about male attitudes toward women back on centre stage, and deals a grievous blow to relations between men and women. It raises questions about violence in society.
>
> At the same time the massacre is said to have had an impact on some men, making them more aware of the feminist case about the massacre's significance, raising their consciousness of the issue and shocking them into reality and action over women's issues. It raises concerns about the engineering profession's image, and puts engineering students' sexist publications in a very different light. It made the

Sun newspaper relegate the third-page female pin-up to the back pages. Finally, the massacre is a mirror reflecting women's experience with male violence and relating it to the struggles of blacks, homosexuals, Jews, and communists. In short, the massacre is credited with producing fear, changing consciousness, demonstrating a pervasive societal pathology, injuring the social fabric, raising questions about professional ethics or public relations, endangering sales, affecting the public political agenda, and revealing a common set of circumstances among otherwise disparate social groups.

If the paraphrase is successful in capturing the variety of functions in one summary statement, it nevertheless does so at the expense of some of the very detail that provides that variety. In addition, then, to appreciating the variety of functions made evident here—from fear inducing to image endangering— it is important to note the *particularity* in the circumstances and content of their formulation. Thus, the women who realize their vulnerability to male violence are not just simply women, but "particularly... those... quite heavily involved in the panty-raid issue" (E123), as well as "two women staying at... [a] shelter for battered women" (E125). It is not just simply women who feel the fear but "residents," "former residents," and "staff" at the shelter (E128). For shelter residents it is not just simply men's violence that they fear but that of "my husband" or "their spouses" (E125, E128). And it is not just simply violence they fear but that "many of their spouses could have, and still could, kill them" (E128).

Similarly, the men whose consciousness has been impacted by the massacre are not just simply men, but "male reporters" (E136), those men "who were already trying to improve gender relationships" (E137), those men "searching for answers to what is being seen as a 'male issue'" (E138). Furthermore, those whose comments are quoted by reporters are not a random collection of commentators, but a relevant collection. We will examine this collection's character in the section after next.

At the same time, of course, these very particulars embody and express generalizations. The "two women" staying at the shelter are, in effect, any two women staying there. It's not specified, particular residents whose vulnerability and fearfulness has been brought out but that of residents in general (E125, E128). It is not separately identified members of staff but staff in general who "now feel the fear too" (E128). It is not particular, named, male reporters whose awareness of the feminist case has been raised but male reporters in general (E136). It is not particular men and women whose relations have been dealt a grievous blow but women and men in general who have suffered this outcome (E134). It is not particular women but women in general to whom there is now "little that is comforting to say" (E126). And so on.

▼

THE MONTREAL MASSACRE AS "SOMETHING FOR US" AND "SOMETHING FOR THEM"

In sociological and criminological accounts of the functions of crime and deviance, functions are specified traditionally with respect to a population; functions are functional for some group or other, even society as a whole. Such a tie between functions and particular categories of recipients was no less in evidence in the formulations of functions contained within our corpus of materials. Accordingly, in this section we consider the categories of person for whom the massacre was said to be functional.

The linkage between functions and categories of recipient (or beneficiary) was achieved via the use of two devices. The first of these refers to the massacre as a "something for us" and the second identifies it as a "something for them." Sacks (1992b: 563) describes the former in the following way:

> And now we get into one of the possibly funny ways that the conversational world operates. There's this thing in the world, "disasters." Except in rather restricted senses "disasters" is not directly a topic in conversation. It can be made into a topic in conversation through various of the means that things can be made topical in conversation. How do you make something topical? One way is to turn it into a "something for us." You can treat it as the most general rule for conversation that people will talk overwhelmingly, not so much about *things* that *happened* to them, but about things *insofar* as they happened to *them*. Talking about whatever, it comes home to us. Which is to say, there are a variety of things happening in the world, like disasters. Their happening doesn't make them introduceable into a conversation. What has to be done is to turn them into something for us.

The "something for us" device for ordering and linking membership categories and consequences was used with respect to a range of categories, ranging from the particular to the general (as we indicated in the previous section). At the particular end of this continuum of categories, "us" and "we" were used to refer to specific recipients of the consequences of the Massacre. These included "those of us...involved in the panty-raid issue" (E123), "residents" and "staff" (at a shelter for battered women) (E128), the engineering profession (E131), and newspaper reporters and editors (E135, E136):

E123   "It made *us* realize how vulnerable *we* are, particularly for *those of us who had been quite heavily involved in the panty-raid issue*, because that debate got quite verbally violent and aggressive, and this threw *us* back to that time," said Sharon Severinski, a graduate student in social work. (*KWR*, Dec 13 [1]; emphasis added)

E128   "*Residents* in the shelter are very upset," Spies said. "It affirms that
many of their spouses could have, and still could, kill them."

Former residents have called, some asking about self-defence
courses, she said. "It's really brought out how vulnerable and fearful they still are."

Staff now feel the fear too, along with residents, said Sue Coulter, public education and volunteer co-ordinator at Anselma House.
"*They are us,*" Coulter said.

...

"But suddenly, and horribly, women have all become acutely aware
of their fear," Coulter said. (*KWR,* Dec 18; emphasis added)

E131   Pierre Belanger, dean of engineering at McGill University, said the
killings nonetheless raise concerns about the *profession's* image.

Sexist publications put out by engineering students at many
universities across the country may no longer be acceptable in this
new environment, he noted, adding that "the massacre puts them
in a very different light." (Dec 12 [4]; emphasis added)

E135   "Yes, *we* have relegated the Sunshine Girl to the back pages, in
light of the enormity of the tragedy and the nature of it," said Sun
associate editor Lorrie Goldstein. (*KWR,* Dec 13 [2]; emphasis
added)

E136   "As far as news content goes, *we* haven't changed anything," Morris said. "I think there's a lot more awareness out there now among
the *male reporters* of the feminist case in this terrible shooting....

"They're looking at the roles of men and women much more
carefully," he said. "But there have been no policy directives at all."
(*KWR,* Dec 13 [2]; emphasis added)

At the general end of the continuum, "us" and "we" were used to refer to "all
of us" (E126) and to "our society" as a whole (E132):

E126   Now there is little that is comforting to say to women. It is a time for
grief for *all of us*; grief for those who have died, and pain at being
reminded of how deep misogyny still runs in *our society*. (Dec 8
[5]; emphasis added)

E132   After the meeting, Mr Mulroney told reporters: "This man singled out
women in a completely criminal and insensitive fashion. It's an isolated incident, but it raises questions about violence in *our society*
and about violence against women." (Dec 8 [2]; emphasis added)

In between these specific and general categories of recipient there are references to "us" and "we" as "women" (E124).

E 124   When these incidents happen "we realize that *as women,* we live
          in bondage in the common fear that we have," Coulter said. "All of
          us have experienced this very personally." (*KWR,* Dec 11 [4]; empha-
          sis added)

The "something for them" device is used alternately and sometimes in
combination with the "something for us" device. Instead of an "us" (or a "we"),
the speaker refers to a "them" for whom the massacre has consequences. The
functions are not formulated by the incumbents of membership categories to
whom they apply but instead by persons who speak on behalf of those for
whom the massacre is seen as functional. The categories for whom and on
whose behalf consequences are formulated via the use of the "something for
them" device range, as with the "something for us" device, from the particular
to the general. They include, particularly, "two women" (residents at a shelter
for battered women) (E 125), "residents" and "former residents" (E 128), and
those "men… who were already trying to improve gender relationships" (E 137):

E 125   *Two women* staying at Anselma House, K-W's shelter for battered
          women and children, were both hit with a sickening realization as
          they watched the lead story on television recently.
               "That could have been my husband doing that to me." (*KWR,*
          Dec 18; emphasis added)

E 128   "*Residents* in the shelter are very upset," Spies said. "It affirms that
          many of their spouses could have, and still could, kill them."
               Former residents have called, some asking about self-defence
          courses, she said. "It's really brought out how vulnerable and fear-
          ful they still are." (*KWR,* Dec 18; emphasis added)

E 137   The shooting has had an impact on some men especially *those
          who were already trying to improve gender relationships,* [Severin-
          ski] said. (*KWR,* Dec 13 [1]; emphasis added)

More general categorial recipients on whose behalf functions are formulated include "women" (E 127, E 128, E 133, E 139), "many women" (E 127, E 128),
"men" and "women" (E 134), "some men," "growing numbers of men" and "the
majority of men" (E 138):

E 127   That was the message that *many women* have received from the
          massacre—a reminder of the violence that *women* face every day,
          the crowd was told (*KWR,* Dec 11, [4]; emphasis added).

E 128   And that's a point, too often missed, in the debate over the impli-
          cations of Lepine's attack on women at the Montreal campus, said
          Paula Caplan, a Toronto psychologist and one of Canada's leading
          feminists.

The point, she said, is that Lepine's rampage with a semi-automatic rifle "echoed" the experiences of *many women* in Canada.

"It rang true for *many, many women.* That's what matters. That's what needs to be recognized. It felt like a shock, but not a surprise." (*KWR,* Dec 18; emphasis added)

E133   Although the speeches steered clear of the panty-raid issue which had earlier rocked the university, people interviewed after the service said the shooting has put the whole debate about male attitudes toward *women* back on centre stage at WLU. (*KWR,* Dec 13 [1]; emphasis added)

E139   [Heald] said *women* can see in the massacre their own personal experience with male violence and can relate it to other struggles in our society—blacks, homosexuals, jews [*sic*] and communists. (*KWR,* Dec 11 [4]; emphasis added)

E134   A Canadian expert on mass murderers says the slayings of 14 women at the University of Montreal last week is "a grievous blow" to relations between *men and women.* (Dec 11 [4]; emphasis added)

E138   The tragedy, so devastating to women who feel vulnerable to violence from men, has also had an impact on some *K-W men searching for answers* to what is being seen as a "male issue."
...

Caplan said *growing numbers of men* have abruptly had their consciousness raised in the wake of the massacre....
...

Caplan said the Montreal massacre has had a stunning impact on *men.*

"*The majority of men* I have heard, and heard about, are saying this has shocked them into reality, over sexual jokes, over their failure to support equal pay legislation, over women's rights to reproductive freedom, and adequate day care."

"It has shocked *them* into action," Caplan said. (*KWR,* Dec 18; emphasis added)

The particular consequences identified also varied according to the category of recipient. Thus, both for women in particular and women in general, the consequences consistently confirmed their experience of male victimization. Thus, they were "reminded," they "realized," they had it "affirmed," it "rang true" and "echoed" their own experience of male violence and male victimization more generally. It could have been their husbands doing it to them. The massacre was a "symbol" of their relations with the men who victimize them. For men, on the other hand, the massacre was said to have had a "stunning impact," it was a "shock," and, for some, it contributed to a "raising of consciousness." Where for women the massacre reminded them of what they already knew, for men it was said to be a learning experience; where for women it confirmed a lifetime of instruction, for men (or at least for some of them) it was instructive. For society (as a whole) the consequence was grief, pain, and a reminder of undesirable societal conditions—widespread misogyny and violence. For particular professional groups (engineers, newspaper reporters, and editors) the massacre was said to raise issues about their professional practices in relation to gender issues.

We will return to the issue of who formulates the consequences of the massacre on behalf of others in the following section of this chapter. For the moment, we will simply emphasize that the "something for us" and the "something for them" devices are not mutually exclusive. They may both be used in the context of a single article and to identify the same recipients. A recipient may be identified as an "us" or as a "them" (e.g., E128 above). Similarly, in the context of a single article the "something for us" device may be used to identify one category of recipient whilst the "something for them" is deployed to refer to another (e.g., E130 above).

The "us," "we," "them," and those who speak on their behalf are quite various, as we have seen. However, the membership categories to which these pro-terms refer also have something recognizably in common. They all belong recognizably to a particular membership categorization device. That is, they are understandably collectible in terms of the device "parties to the social problem of the male victimization of women." These parties include not only female victims and male victimizers but, as we have seen, women and men more generally, social work students, chaplains, psychologists, anthropologists, feminists, experts on gender relations, sociologists, local activists, public education coordinators, counsellors, politicians and political activists, government officials, and so forth. Their membership of this collection is determined not only by their co-incumbency of the category "victim" but by their having particular interests in, expertise with respect to, or contributions to make to this particular problem. This device, then, provides the organizational parameters for selecting particular categories of person to formulate the consequences of the massacre. It is to this issue that we now turn, in the final section of this chapter.

▼
FUNCTIONS AND FORMULATORS

As we stated above in the section on members' formulations of the functions of the massacre, our third analytic issue concerns the noticeably unremarkable collection of identities of those who come to be selected by media personnel to formulate and express the massacre's consequences for those constituencies.

The list of women, residents, and staff of a shelter for battered women, feminists, psychologists, counsellors, education officers, chaplains, anthropologists, sociologists, politicians, and political activists appear as a "natural" collection, even if they are, as it were, occasioned together by the massacre itself. It is to this issue that we now turn.

As we examine this we will take up for particular scrutiny a remarkable passage by Sacks (1992b: 194–195) in which he considers the integrative functions of crime and public disasters:

> There is a phenomenon that's been widely observed: In times of public disaster and tragedy people in large cities who otherwise do not talk to each other, develop "comeraderie," [*sic*] talk to each other.... We have to try to develop some sort of explanations, characterizations, of why that happens....
>
> Let's consider some things about the situation of "strangers" in the streets of cities.... I mentioned the status of the crowd outside of Bullocks [a department store], and said that a thing about the occurrence of a crowd around, say, a possible crime [presence of police car outside of department store], is that somebody who sees the crowd and the crime, sees what the crowd is looking at, whereas otherwise what anybody is looking at in the streets is not available. With that, we can achieve a small part of the sense of what is called the "integrative function of crime," i.e., in such a situation you know what's on all these people's minds.
>
> We can in similar fashion get at the integrative functions of disaster and tragedy. That is, it is otherwise routinely nobody's business on the one hand and perhaps unsolvable on the other, what's on the mind of the person who's passing you. Furthermore, it's your business to not make it their business as to what's on your mind by doing something which would cause them to wonder what's on that person's mind, e.g., by crying in the streets. Crying in the streets is not a thing that somebody's encountering somebody doing it can solve—except classificatorily, e.g., they can say it's some private problem—and it's something you shouldn't cause them to try to solve. But at least one facet of the integrative status of public tragedy is that somebody standing on the street can cry, and the set of persons who pass him, who don't know him, can know what he's crying about, i.e., he's crying about that public event. Your mind is, then, made available to the anonymous persons who encounter you, who otherwise have it as not their business to figure it out, and who otherwise can't.
>
> So, a sort of thing that happens in public disasters is that persons can express emotions in public places, and those emotions are available to others, who need not avoid looking at the person who's sad, and also can figure that they know why he's sad.

In this connection, Sacks speaks of "intimacy" and reminds us that this involves "doing firsts that are not tied to prior matters." That is, it turns out that we have an item that we can do with strangers: we can be "intimate" with strangers; we can speak about our emotions without being invited to do so. Put more technically, we can treat disasters in particular ways that presume the operational relevance of a we-relationship to the disaster. Such a we-relationship, we can say, implies a membership collection or categorization device such as "parties to a public disaster." That we can then talk in intimate ways, in those terms, rather than in other more reserved and formal ways, presumes the operational relevance of those particular category relations. It is therefore possible to document the ways in which disasters are treated in ways that presume the operational relevance of a we-relationship to the disaster.

Several features of our materials are accountable in terms of these kinds of considerations. As we have shown in the previous section, a we-relationship is consistently invoked in the quotations and commentaries regarding the consequences of the massacre. Thus, with respect to the question—under what auspices can persons speak and act in relation to the massacre—we can say that it is not just under the auspices of "R" (an intimate relationship to the deceased) that persons may "grieve" and "mourn" their "tragic loss," but that "outrage," "sadness," "anger," etc., are, by virtue of the public character of the massacre, or by virtue of their being tied to that event, tellable (that is, observable-reportable) matters. And indeed when the news stories are told, as we have seen, many make reference to the parties to the event engaging in appropriate, that is, category-bound activities of various kinds. Parties are reported as crying, for example. Indeed, in terms of the viewer's maxim, in the doing of such activities and in the reports of them, they can be seen as such parties. So, the occurrence of the various stories (tragedy, horror, etc.), or rather their social organization, is a matter of the categorial connections between (a) the character of the event and (b) the ordinarily permissible, category-bound activities of "parties to a public disaster." This is really the issue of who gets to tell the functions, and who gets to tell is a matter of who can speak. Permission is a category predicate.

However, there is a more particular categorial connection between the formulations of functions and the massacre than the device "parties to a public disaster." It is not just anyone, any stranger off the street, who is interviewed, quoted, and included for commentary. Rather, particular selections appear to have been made. That this is so, of course, is unsurprising in that an aspect of our common-sense knowledge of society is that knowledge itself is not distributed evenly amongst the members of society. Particular kinds of knowledge are predicated of, even owned (Sharrock 1974) by, certain membership categories. Accordingly, when people require advice or a specific kind of service, particular categories of person are appropriate to turn to, as it were (cf. Sacks, 1967, 1972). It is therefore unsurprising that a particular array of category incumbents were selected by the news media for consultation and quotation in the (category-generated) context of the story of the social problem of male victimization of women as the predominant story of the Montreal Massacre. The story of the functions is accomplished in part, then, by selecting persons who stand in a particular relationship to the massacre. There is, in other words, a discernible consistency in the membership categories of those who are selected for quotation and commentary regarding the functions of the Montreal Massacre. They can all be understood, as we have already suggested in the previous section, to be incumbents of the membership categorization device "parties to the social problem of the victimization of women." Thus, we showed in the previous section how one of the "parties" to the disaster, namely, co-incumbents or fellow victims who fit into the categories made available by the killings, gets to speak of the consequences of the killings. Their speech, their entitlement to formulate functions, derives from their particular category relationship to the killings. Other parties who get to formulate functions are those who count themselves, and are counted by others, as speaking on behalf of the victims of the *Montreal Massacre* in particular and women victims of male violence in general. Their speech is occasioned by their membership of other relevant categories such as "feminist," "social worker," "local activist," "sociologist," "leading expert on ...," "feminist psychologist," and so forth. Similarly, politicians and political activists, as parties to (the politics) of the social problem of the *Montreal Massacre*, can make political talk about the issues involved for them. So, the character of their speech and their selection to speak in the first place involves not simply their presence on the streets at a time of public tragedy or their "public" membership of society but their relationship to the issues raised by the killings (or more specifically by the media treatment of them). Their talk is not just about death—people die, hence we express and are exhorted to express grief and pain—but it is also about a social and political problem. That is, *because* it is seen as a social and political problem, it occasions report, quotation, and commentary on just that problem. Clearly, in addition, the speech that formulates the functions of the massacre reflexively constitutes the character of its treatment as a social problem.

The question that motivates analysis is: what provides for these people talking in the first place? In another context, Sacks (1967, 1972) talks about what provides for the propriety of calls to a Suicide Prevention Centre. It is the person's category membership as one who "has no one to turn to" that provides for such calls. In our materials it is the speakers' co-membership of the device "parties to the social problem of the male victimization of women" that provides for their talk.

▼
CONCLUDING REMARKS

It is not only that the speakers who get to speak are appropriate speakers by virtue of their co-membership of the device "parties to the social problem of the male victimization of women." In addition, their formulation of the functions is likewise hearably appropriate. Not only are they proper persons, given the organization of media reportage and commentary on the *Montreal Massacre* as an instance of the social problem of male victimization of women, but also what is said is similarly proper. Both the public disaster and the particular social problem itself provide, in other words, a *place* for appropriate expressions and responses, including not only sorrow, grief, and pain on the part of "anyone" but also the kinds of responses predicated of the parties who were selected to speak. These questions of proper response also raised personal issues for us, and it is to these that we turn in the last chapter.

CHAPTER 8

Conclusion: Ethnomethodology, Moral Order, and Membership Categorization Analysis

▼
INTRODUCTION

In this book we have used an ethnomethodological approach to analyze media coverage of the murders that became known as the Montreal Massacre. In chapters 2, 3, and 4 we considered the reportage, while in chapters 5, 6, and 7 we have been principally occupied with aspects of the media commentary. In our preface to this book we also noted that in the course of our work we came to reflect on our own personal experience of, and position with respect to, various aspects of our phenomenon. In this concluding discussion it is to these personal issues that we wish to turn. We do this not because we have any interest in aligning ourselves via public confession or self-advertisement with the positions made available by these aspects, nor because we wish to join our preceding analyses with the dimensions of moral or political debates about, for example, violence against women or gun control. Rather, we address these issues because we have found it instructive to reflect upon them in the light of our analytic orientation.

We mentioned in our preface that our phenomenon was a perspicuous one. By this we mean in part that it affords an exemplary case of how social phenomena are unavoidably made available in and as their description, and in the preceding chapters we have sought to analyze the various ways our phenomenon was thereby made available in and as its media reportage and commentary. Our phenomenon is also perspicuous in a second sense. Thus, although the task we had set ourselves was an ethnomethodological one, we nevertheless found ourselves relating to our materials in other than ethnomethodological terms. For us, as for others, the Montreal Massacre *was* a crime, it *was* horrific, it *was* a tragedy, it *was* violence against women, it *was* misogyny taken to horrendously extreme lengths, and so forth. No amount of ethnomethodological indifference prevented us from experiencing the event as reported in these ways. In terms of the horrendous objectivity of the murders, then, we also came to experience certain emotional responses to the media reports; we found ourselves engaged emotionally with the phenomenon as described and represented in the media reportage and commentary. Sympathy, sorrow, despair, dismay, guilt, and anger all surfaced in our reflections and conversations at one time or another. As we became increasingly familiar with our data and, in particular, with the grief and anguish not only of those who were related to the immediate victims but also of those who saw themselves as victims of men's violence, we found ourselves almost irretrievably drawn into the moral and political dimensions of the event and the wider problem it was so convincingly portrayed as being a part of. We were, then, not mere onlookers, nor just analysts, because we too were appalled by the event and the wider range of violence against women to which it belonged. We were drawn into the dimensions of the event as it was presented to the public in the news reports. Scenes of victims, police, ambulance workers, and feminist and pro-feminist commentators all invite, as it were, "natural" responses, not analytic ones. Ours were naturally forthcoming.

We also found ourselves wondering about the appropriateness of our research in the light of our phenomenon's horrendous objectivity. It was thus just a short step from our emotional response to self-doubt about our analytic approach. We found ourselves thinking and talking about the possibility that somehow our analytical response was inadequate, that our inquiry should have engaged morally and politically with this atrocity and embodied a side-taking in the moral and political dimensions made available by our materials. At such turning points we might have been inclined to throw in the towel of analysis, take up the messy morality business and take sides in the dirty war between good and evil. We knew, of course, that there would be objections to our kind of work from those who prefer to argue that the point of inquiry is not to describe or understand the world but to change it. We knew too that such a critical orientation enjoys widespread acceptance (in various guises) amongst our colleagues in the social sciences. Wherever there are morally and politically objectionable forms of human suffering, then, so the argument might go, it is the obligation, even responsibility, of the intellectual to work towards its alleviation through social change.[1]

These uncomfortable emotions, reflections, and temptations were compounded when we attempted to present a version of chapter 4 to an academic audience at a small conference on gender and theory. Thus, the presenter was asked to provide the good of the analysis-and-presentation in the following sense: what could the analysis offer that would justify putting the predominantly female audience through the pain and discomfort of having to confront the killer again in the form of his suicide letter and announcement at the scene? For, following ethnomethodological precedent, the data were made available to the audience as handouts and overheads so they could check the analysis themselves. The question, that is, was one posed in terms of what might be called the "moral-emotional economy" of inquiry. Does the good of the analysis outweigh the moral-emotional costs? The presentation was, in fact, interrupted early on and the presenter asked to provide our conclusions so that the audience could weigh that question. Following that assessment it would be decided if the presenter should continue. Discussion ensued for at least half an hour, ably managed by the conference hosts. The presenter, indeed, refused to continue until there was agreement that he should. At some point into the discussion, and with considerable consternation, the presenter complied with the request to provide the conclusions. Some sort of resolution was reached. Nobody walked out (as far as the presenter recalls). The paper was then read to the end.

During the discussion, the suicide letter was characterized as, or as like, hate literature. It was likened, that is, to such other noxious documents as *The Protocols of the Elders of Zion* or *Mein Kampf* or, according to some forms of feminist analysis, some forms of pornography. In that sense, it invited entry into debates over free speech, censorship, and the like. One salient feminist contribution to such debates has been to insist on a measure of harm being incorporated into the assessment of the legitimacy of forms of questionable speech. It was precisely such a demand that was being pressed on the occasion in question.[2]

The additional perspicuity of our phenomenon, then, would appear to lie in how it affords the opportunity for reflection on our work as a response to *these* features of the phenomenon, to the phenomenon understood *as* criminal, *as* horrific, *as* tragic, *as* violently anti-women, *as* a case of counter-revolutionary terrorism, and so forth. Our question, then, is what then were we to do with these emotions and this response? Our answer is that whilst it is easy to endorse these dimensions of the event as represented in the media treatment of it, and whilst we did find ourselves doing precisely this, our preference here is not to revise our analyses in the light of such reconsiderations nor is it to recommend a combination of ethnomethodological and politically motivated inquiry. In the following section we outline our rationale for this answer.

▼

ETHNOMETHODOLOGY AND THE MORAL ORDER OF EMOTIONAL AND POLITICAL RESPONSE

One reason why we have not taken a side, as it were, is because we do not wish to confuse our sociological (ethnomethodological) analysis with our personal feelings about or our political position with respect to the murders. We mentioned earlier that one possible objection to our kind of inquiry is derived from the position that the point of inquiry is not so much to understand the world but to change it. In response to those who claim that inquiry *must* be politically oriented, *must* engage with the moral dimensions of phenomena, it is our argument that any proposal for change presupposes a *description* of *what* is in need of change, and any description will have been produced by the parties to it with the use of members' methods. For us, then, and for ethnomethodology in general, there is a prior investigative task to be accomplished, namely, the analysis of how descriptions of social phenomena are produced in the first place.

Furthermore, insofar as our ethnomethodological stance involves a commitment to a particular kind of inquiry, then there can only be confusion in seeking to harness it or combine it with an orientation grounded in an entirely different set of auspices. Thus, although we have no wish to deny or resist our experience of the horrendous objectivity of the murders, nevertheless, analytically speaking, what is interesting is *how* horrendousness, as one feature of a phenomenon, is accomplished in and through its description. Consequently, to shift analytic attention at this point would be confusing in that it would presume the character of the thing being described. Yet this is precisely what we have sought to make problematic. It would, then, involve a kind of surrender to the tyranny of the object, to its overwhelming mundaneity (Pollner 1987). Our interest, as we stated at the outset, is in the *Montreal Massacre* as a *members'* phenomenon. In this regard we differentiated in chapter 1 the focus of ethnomethodology from those found in realist and social constructionist approaches to crime and deviance. Hence our analytic topic has been the description and treatment of the Montreal Massacre *by members*, not its horrendous objectivity *for us*. If we presumed for the sake of inquiry its objective character, then there would be no point in doing ethnomethodology in the first place.

One way, then, of handling these kinds of objections involves a clear-sighted adherence to the auspices of our approach, and thereby separating ethnomethodological inquiry on the one hand from politically motivated inquiry on the other.[3] Another, more important reason for sustaining our ethnomethodological point of view is that it allows us to understand the production, in the first place, of our emotional responses and any subsequent self-doubt about the proper course of inquiry in relation to it. Accordingly, our inclination is to see our emotional response and any self-doubt about the appropriateness of ethnomethodological inquiry in the face of a disturbing and distressing phenomenon, not as a pretext for a different kind of inquiry but as an opportunity for analysis. In other words, for us, then, every occasion of sense and action provides an opportunity for analysis. Where that sense or action happens to be our own, it affords an opportunity for analysis of a self-reflective kind. Rather than abandoning our analytic orientation in favour of the point of view under whose auspices our emotions and subsequent doubt about the moral/political appropriateness of our approach were generated, we instead seek to understand such genesis in terms of our analytic orientation.

How then are our emotional responses and indeed our self-doubt about the morality of our inquiry to be understood? Our answer is that both our emotional responses and any sense of unease about our work were both products of a members' approach to the phenomenon. More particularly, they were account-able in the terms of precisely the same ethnomethodological orientation that we had used to analyze our materials in the first place, namely membership cat-egorization analysis. Thus, in general, our responses can be understood as having been produced because we were members of society. More particu-larly, we suggest that our emotional responses—and any doubts we had about whether our mode of intellectual engagement was proper and responsible—can be understood as having been generated in terms of membership cate-gories and category predicates made relevant by the media reportage and commentary, that is to say, certain membership categories and their predi-cates that were touched off by our phenomenon.

When it comes to making sense of and responding to social phenomena we are, to put it plainly, not just ethnomethodologists. We are also fathers and sons, husbands and lovers, friends and foes, professors and colleagues, to name just a few amongst a whole host of other memberships, some fleeting, some recurrent, some claimed, some disputed, some imputed and some denied, yet all locally and occasionally expressed. Few, if any, of these member-ships are omnirelevant. Rather, they *become* relevant. Categories and their predicates are locally ordered. Certain arrangements, relationships, actions, and events *make them relevant.* Furthermore, as incumbents of these various categories, we are entitled and obliged to engage in activities predicated of them, to display associated and/or constitutive attributes and perhaps to have certain attitudes, beliefs, opinions, thoughts, and feelings.

More particularly, for a given *members'* characterization of an event there are normatively arranged, organizationally provided for, categorially built, paired responses. Such responses appear on cue, just like the characters who appeared in chapter 2. Indeed, their non-appearance is an accountable mat-ter. Furthermore, insofar as these pairings are normatively and serially ordered, they display organizational features similar to those of adjacency pairs in con-versation. First one thing occurs, then another, the second ordered relative to the first. The production of the first makes relevant the production of the sec-ond, such that when it is not forthcoming, it is noticeably absent.

Such relative ordering and conditional relevance pertains to news report and news receipt. We suggest, first of all, that the category of news implies the character of the response to it. The response to good news is conventionally dif-ferent from that to bad news.[4] It is beyond the scope of this discussion to address this in any rigorous way with respect to naturally occurring conversa-tional data, but it seems at least intuitively the case that certain kinds of good news will be received in a congratulatory manner. A: "I'm getting married." B: "Really? Congratulations!" the sequence might go, or, A: "I passed my exams." B: "Great. Well done." Contrastively, we know that the grammar of bad news makes relevant acts of commiseration. The conventional response to news of a death in the family, for example, is an expression of sympathy, as in, A: "My mother died." B: "Oh, I'm sorry to hear that." Alternatively put, the category of news proffered makes relevant different (membership) categories of response. To the recently engaged we are congratulators, to the bereaved we are commiserators, to the distraught we are comforters, and so forth.

Several features of these action-category pairs can be noted. First, their second pair parts, as it were, are produced on cue. Their appearance does not have to be explained; no special motive is required to understand how it is that sad news is met with commiseration or happy news with celebration. It is, then, and second, utterly unsurprising when these interactional events occur in this way. Third, they are also normatively ordered pairings. That is, when the "proper" response is not forthcoming, it is noticeably absent. The receipt of tragic news is appropriately in the form of commiseration rather than non-chalance or indifference. The non-appearance of commiseration is a noticeable and accountable matter. The non-commiserating recipient of tragic news is rendered vulnerable to description as possibly unsympathetic, insensitive, or worse. Likewise, we are naturally appalled at the news of a horrific accident accompanied, say, by pictures of gore, carnage, rubble, and broken bodies. Expressions of shock appear on cue. "How terrible," we say. The alternative, "how wonderful," would be odd indeed except perhaps when we take the victims being categorized to be the "enemy," but then that is another story.

Our emotional responses to the murders comprising the Montreal Massacre can, then, be understood as having been categorially ordered in this way, as having been produced under the auspices of membership categories such as these. It is in this sense that we were "caught in the web" of description. As members, we had little choice, it seemed, but to respond in these ways. That is, the media reportage of and commentary on the Montreal Massacre made relevant particular categorially organized responses on our part as news recipients or more specifically as parties to news reports about the Montreal Massacre. These category-relevant responses are touched off by the news reports and commentaries. Our materials provide for our category membership not just as newspaper reader, nor news recipient. Rather, just as a description of tragedy invites our sympathy, so a description of, or commentary on, violence against women invites our alignment with one side or the other. The moral dimensions invoked in the media descriptions invite us as readers to participate in a morality play. Where the public identity of the event is largely a political one, then it is unsurprising that we are drawn into its range.

When somebody dies in a tragic accident or, as in this case, when a number of women are brutally murdered, an expression of sympathy will be noticeable in its absence. To express sorrow and sadness for the victims and their families is a normal, natural emotional response to such an experience. There is a formal categorial machinery in play here. It is a tragedy, so we respond with sympathy and commiseration. We are sympathizers and commiserators relationally paired with the victims of tragedy. It is horrific, so we express our shock and revulsion. These emotional responses demonstrate and constitute our participation in the local culture of tragic and horrific news. Conversely, not to have responded in these ways could have been seen to mark our cultural estrangement.

As we have seen, the media commentary gave extensive coverage to the view that the murders were part of a larger problem of violence against women. As such, the media made relevant our taking a position on *this* issue. We suggest that our response here reflects our category membership. Thus, just as the description, "Abraham the Hebrew," is indicative of the category membership of its user (Sacks 1992a: 171, 397), so also does our response to the Montreal Massacre reflect our category membership. It is indeed a feature of a common-sense knowledge, furthermore, that different responses are predicated of different categories. There is, in other words, scope for alternative responses with some categories of events and, most relevantly, events categorizable as moral or political. A news report that the Conservative Party has lost all its seats may be received by either irrepressible joy or suicidal gloom, depending on one's point of view, one's category membership. Similarly we may suppose that a co-counterrevolutionary, a fanatical anti-feminist, might have congratulated Lépine for his deeds. By the same token, then, our particular responses are understandable in terms of our category memberships.

Political actors, and especially political activists, are not only entitled to but would indeed be expected to have an opinion on the events in question. As members of a political party, as human rights activists, as anarchists, as liberals, as conservatives, and so forth, we might be expected to have a view, an opinion about an event with such transparently moral and political features. Such opinions will appear on cue and, indeed, when they do not so appear, will be noticeably absent. Indeed, not to have such an opinion, not to proffer a timely view might, at least in political circles, be sufficient for others to call into question one's credentials *as* a political actor.

Neither of us pretends, being men, that we know what it is to be literally or metaphorically a woman in the gunsight of a very angry white male. However, one of us is a human rights activist with respect to a number of issues, including pro-feminist ones, and both of us would categorize ourselves as on the side of women's equality. Such category memberships make understandable our being appalled by, and our sense of opposition and anger towards, the Marc Lépines of this world and what they are said to represent. This is because such responses are predicates of these membership categories. Again, for us, as incumbents of categories such as these, our responses appear on cue.

Our misgivings about the appropriate analytical response are understandable in a similar way. To the extent that we shared their grief or their politics, we might want to even go so far as to conduct our inquiries and write our reports in such a way that they coincided with those members' views with whom we sympathized. Particular category affiliations, in other words, can provide for a keen sense of duty, obligation, moral rectitude, and political direction. A human rights activist or self-avowed feminist sociologist, for example, can properly have qualms about a form of inquiry that did not have as its *sine qua non* the correction of perceived injustices. For such a member, much of social life will be viewed in terms of its moral and political choices. Incumbency of the category of human rights activist entails a pervasive enjoinder to act politically. It is therefore unsurprising that ethnomethodology would then be called into question since it is not, after all, an activity predicated of political activist or human rights activist.[5]

▼
CONCLUDING REMARKS

In chapter 7 we respecified the social functions of crime argument by considering those functions as a members' phenomenon. If our being drawn into the various aspects of the phenomenon is understood in the way identified above, we can say also that it serves as confirmation of media's role in relation to the functions of crime and the maintenance of moral boundaries. Thus, to revisit the quotation from Sacks (1992b: 194) on the integrative functions of crime and public disasters from the previous chapter:

> There is a phenomenon that's been widely observed: In times of public disaster and tragedy people in large cities who otherwise do not talk to each other, develop "comaraderie," [*sic*] talk to each other.... We have to try to develop some sorts of explanations, characterizations, of why that happens....
>
> Let's consider some things about the situation of "strangers" in the streets of the cities.... I mentioned the status of the crowd outside of Bullocks [a department store], and said that a thing about the occurrence of a crowd around, say, a possible crime, is that somebody who sees the crowd and the crime, sees what the crowd is looking at, whereas otherwise what anybody is looking at in the streets is not available. With that, we can achieve a small part of the sense of what is called the "integrative function of crime," i.e., in such a situation you know what's on all these people's minds.
>
> We can in similar fashion get at the integrative function of disaster and tragedy. That is, it is otherwise routinely nobody's business on the one hand, and perhaps unsolvable on the other, what's on the mind of the person who's passing you. Furthermore, it's your business to not make it their business as to what's on your mind....

> So, a sort thing that happens in public disasters is that persons can express emotions in public places, and those emotions are available to others.... Public tragedies, then, make persons' emotions publicly available and publicly explainable to anonymous parties. Also, persons can express emotions in public without having that they are doing that treated as something embarrassing, something they shouldn't do, etc.

What is so remarkable about these observations of Sacks is that for the first time they seek to address the detail of what it means to say that the members of society can be integrated by crime or disaster reports. Picking up Sacks's point about knowing what's on other people's minds, part of the problem for us was that we knew what was on all these other people's minds (and, as we have seen, some of them told us so). That is, we knew they weren't puzzled about it intellectually in the way that we were, and we knew they were, in various ways emotional about it. They were angry, they were sad and upset. Indeed, the news media told us so. The "stories" we have presented were the ways in which the murders were treated: as crime, as horror, as tragedy, etc. What was on others' minds, then, insofar as this was made available by the news media, was the horror, tragedy, etc. Indeed, so powerful were these integrative currents that we even came to feel that it is an accountable matter that we did not say where we stood, that we were not sharing in these stories. It was for this reason that we wondered what our work had to do with these public expressions of emotion. In this way, we, as members, are like the parties to a public disaster described by Sacks. Not only are we entitled to speak to strangers about our emotions in relation to such events but such emotions are expectably available for others; they appear expectably on cue. Furthermore, when they are found absent, they are an accountable matter: the persons who do not share in the common grief are not only different, odd, and outside the integrated ones, they are also endowed with qualities that express their indifference and opposition to the expected responses, to the community that is invoked by the collective emotional outpouring.

The media-mediated categorizations became the discourse for our thoughts. As such, we might say that we were part of the integrative process in which the media are supposedly functional. Our inclinations were to join with others and speak with them as members and as such were integrated by the media. Further, to the extent that we, as members, shared with other members, represented by the media, a sense of loss or outrage, then it would seem reasonable that we should let those members know what was on our minds. In this small and intricate, seen but unnoticed way, our social integration was methodically accomplished. It has been, throughout, a story of membership categorization analysis.

And yet, as we have indicated in this concluding discussion, we have resisted the invitation contained in the integrative currents of the categorial organization of the Montreal Massacre. We have sought to remain detached, as it were, even from our own emotions and political commitments, and have sought to reflect upon their organization. Perhaps it is through self-reflection on the socially organized grounds of our emotional and moral reasoning that the violent excesses they seem to sometimes permit can be avoided.

Appendix

IN THE TEXT WE PRESENT the data in the form of numbered extracts (for example, E1) consisting of a part or the whole of an article. In one case, a whole article is presented in the form of a separate figure. Each article is itself identified by its date of publication together with a number. In the case of the *Kitchener-Waterloo Record* we add the prefix *KWR* to distinguish its articles from those in the *Globe and Mail*. The numbers simply distinguish the different articles published on our topic on that day. The order of the numbers generally reflects the order of appearance of the articles in the paper; that is, for example [2] appears either on the same page as, or on a later page, than [1]. Some of the *KWR* citations have no number, as we referred to one article only from the paper for that day. The following lists give, for each paper, in chronological order, the title, byline, and page number of each article according to its date and number in the text. Where an article appeared on the front page, we indicate whether or not it was the lead article. In a page number like, for example, A7, the A refers to the main news section of the paper; a B refers to the Local section of the *Kitchener-Waterloo Record*; a D refers to the Focus section of the Saturday *Globe and Mail*, which contains major feature articles and editorials. Bold face indicates that the original headline was either in particularly large type or particularly bold face or both. Underlining indicates underlining in the original, while italics indicate a slanted typeface in the original.

▼
THE *GLOBE AND MAIL*

Dec 7 [1]   **"Man in Montreal kills 14 with rifle,"** Canadian Press and Staff, Montreal, front page (lead article).

Dec 7 [2]   "Terrified students describe shooting scene," Canadian Press, Montreal, page A5.

Dec 8 [1]   **"Killer's letter blames feminists** / *Suicide note contains apparent hit list of 15 women,"* by Victor Malarek, the *Globe and Mail*, Montreal, front page (lead article).

Dec 8 [2]   "Quebec mourns senseless deaths," by Patricia Poirier and Barrie McKenna, the *Globe and Mail*, Montreal, front page.

Dec 8 [3]   "Why were women in the gunsight?" Editorial, page A6.

Dec 8 [4]   "The massacre in Montreal / **Speaking about the unspeakable**," by Emil Sher, Mr. Sher is a Montreal writer, Montreal, page A7.

Dec 8 [5]   "A time for grief and pain," by Diana Bronson. Ms Bronson is a Montreal journalist who wrote the following commentary for CBC Radio's *Morningside* program, Montreal, page A7.

Dec 8 [6]   "Systematic slaughter is without precedent," MICHAEL VALPY, page A8.

Dec 8 [7]   *"Hundreds in Toronto mourn killing of 14 women,"* by Stevie Cameron, page A13.

Dec 8 [8]   "Opposition MPs demand long-promised gun control," by Richard Cleroux and Craig McInnes, the *Globe and Mail*, Ottawa, page A13.

Dec 8 [9]   "Police suspected more than 1 sniper was loose in school," by Benoit Aubin, the *Globe and Mail* with Canadian Press, Montreal, page A13.

Dec 8 [10] "Mass murders not increasing, Canadian anthropologist says," by Robert MacLeod, page A13.

Dec 8 [11] *"Canada's past includes other mass shootings,"* Canadian Press, page A13.

Dec 8 [12] "14 dead women identified," Canadian Press, Montreal, page A13.

Dec 9 [1]   *"Don't have feelings of guilt, woman hurt in massacre urges her fellow students,"* by Benoit Aubin, the *Globe and Mail*, Montreal, front page.

Dec 9 [2]   *"Violent film on terrorists preceded tragedy,"* Canadian Press, Montreal, page A6.

Dec 9 [3]   "*Killer fraternized with men in army fatigues,"* by Victor Malarek, the *Globe and Mail*, Montreal, page A6.

Dec 9 [4]   "Lewis will not commit to tough 1978 gun law that wasn't proclaimed," by Graham Fraser, the *Globe and Mail*, Ottawa, page A6.

Dec 9 [5]   "**OUR DAUGHTERS, OURSELVES**," by Stevie Cameron, page D1.

Dec 9 [6]   "Violence and anger," WORD PLAY by John Allemang, page D6.

Dec 11 [1] "Thousands of mourners wait in silence to pay final respects to slain women," Staff and Canadian Press, Montreal, front page.

Dec 11 [2] "Aware of symbolism," letter to the editor, page A6.

Dec 11 [3] "Litany of social ills created Marc Lepine," MICHAEL VALPY page A8.

Dec 11 [4] "Slayings deal blow to gender relations, murder expert says," Staff and Canadian Press, page A9.

Dec 11 [5]　*"Families, friends remember victims' lives,"* Canadian Press, Montreal, page A9.

Dec 11 [6]　"Ease of getting gun in Canada 'unacceptable,' Mulroney says," the *Globe and Mail*, Meech Lake, Que., page A9.

Dec 12 [1]　"3,500 friends, relatives bid a tearful farewell to murdered students," by Victor Malarek, the *Globe and Mail*, Montreal, front page.

Dec 12 [2]　"**'Men cannot know the feelings of fear'**" / Yet an anti-feminist backlash has been intensified by the massacre in Montreal," by Melanie Randall. Ms Randall is a doctoral student in political science at York University and a researcher-activist in the field of women and violence, page A7.

Dec 12 [3]　"More massacre details to be released by police, but an inquiry ruled out," by Victor Malarek, the *Globe and Mail* with Canadian Press, Montreal, page A14.

Dec 12 [4]　"Quebec engineers observe day of mourning," by Barrie McKenna, the *Globe and Mail*, Montreal, page A14.

Dec 12 [5]　"Tension grows at Queen's over sexism controversy," by Stevie Cameron and Orland French, the *Globe and Mail*, page A14.

Dec 12 [6]　"Risk of murder linked to non-domestic roles," MICHAEL VALPY, A8.

Dec 13 [1]　"Police refusal to answer questions leaves lots of loose ends in killings," by Victor Malarek, the *Globe and Mail*, Montreal, page A18.

Dec 13 [2]　*"1,000 fill church in Montreal to mourn victim of massacre,"* by Patricia Poirier, the *Globe and Mail*, Montreal, page A18.

Dec 13 [3]　"Students' newspaper warned to end sexism," by Orland French, the *Globe and Mail*, page A18.

Dec 16 [1]　"The self-centred hype of Montreal massacre," LISE BISSONNETTE, page D2.

▼

KITCHENER-WATERLOO RECORD (KWR)

Dec 7 [1]　"**Killer hated women** / 14 dead in rampage at college," by Penn MacRae, The Canadian Press, Montreal, front page (lead article).

Dec 7 [2]　"'Joke' turns into terror / 'It was a human hunt, we were the quarry,'" Montreal (CP), front page.

Dec 7 [3]　"Last day of classes suddenly shattered," by Andrew McIntosh, *Montreal Gazette*, Montreal, page A5.

Dec 7 [4]　"Policeman finds body of daughter," Montreal (CP), page A5.

Dec 7 [5]　"Justice consultant urges stricter gun control laws," Ottawa (CP), page A5.

Dec 9 [1]　"300 at Guelph ceremony mourn death of students," by Margaret Mironowicz, *Record* staff, Guelph, front page.

Dec 9 [2]   "TV aired movie of terror in the classroom," Montreal (CP), page A8.

Dec 11 [1]   "Canada grieves brutal killings / 10,000 pay respects in Montreal," Record wire services, page A1.

Dec 11 [2]   "Marc Lepine: abused child who grew up to be a quitter," Montreal (CP), page A8.

Dec 11 [3]   "Priest confesses shame over 14 slain," by Margaret Mironowicz, *Record* staff, Cambridge, page B1.

Dec 11 [4]   "100 attend Speaker's Corners vigil for 14 women slain in Montreal," by Monica Gutschi, *Record* staff, page B3.

Dec 12 [1]   "Mourners see better world / Massacre debated as 14 buried," Montreal (CP), front page.

Dec 12 [2]   "Grieving together," Editorial, page A6.

Dec 12 [3]   "Massacre proves need for ban on automatic guns," Christopher Young, Ottawa, page A6.

Dec 12 [4]   "'He'd never ask for help' / The murderer of 14 university women grew up with a brutal father," by Rod MacDonell, Elizabeth Thompson, Andrew McIntosh, and William Marsden, Montreal, page A7.

Dec 13 [1]   "Killings rekindle panty-raid debate," by Rose Simone, *Record* staff, B1.

Dec 13 [2]   "Girl photos bumped to back pages by shooting," by Chisholm Macdonald, The Canadian Press, page A12.

Dec 14   "Universities honor 14 dead / Hatred continues, UW service told," by Margaret Mironowicz, *Record* staff, page B1.

Dec 18   "Montreal massacre shocks men into action," by Margaret Mironowicz, *Record* staff, page B1.

Dec 29   "Montreal slayings seen as random violent acts," Toronto (CP), front page.

Notes

▼
CHAPTER 1

1 Please see the Appendix for the conventions used in citing the news articles which comprise, save for Lépine's suicide letter, the entire corpus of materials on which this study is based. Also, according to the Publisher's Note in *The Montreal Massacre* (Malette and Chalouh 1991: [9]), "the reaction in Quebec, and specifically in the French-language media, is of great interest because it differs from reaction in the English-language media." We would be interested to see if such differences are reproduced by an analysis of the French-language media (by a knowledgeable French-speaking colleague) corresponding to the categorizational analysis we attempt here.

2 This claim may strike readers as controversial insofar as a common complaint on the part of feminists was that, to quote again the Publisher's Note in the principal source on the massacre, "while the mainstream media scrambled to ignore or downplay the significance of the victims being women, the analysis of feminists was ignored or ridiculed or rejected with hostility" (Malette and Chalouh 1991: [9]). The complaint is repeated by Mahood (1996: 367), and similar claims are made by Bart and Moran (1993: xiii) and Meyers (1997: 11). We consider them in more detail in note 2 of chapter 5. It should be added that the author of the aforesaid Publisher's Note is prepared to allow that "the English-language media, perhaps because of its relative distance from the event, allowed more information to filter through to the public"; nevertheless, "it too lacked the courage to step out of its role as the reflector of an essentially misogynist and patriarchal point of view" (Malette and Chalouh 1991: [9]).

3 A further argument for this position is that any theory of the media presupposes a knowledge of how the media work. But for us, what is readily observable is that members consume the media—in our case, read the papers—without benefit of instruction in any theory of the media. Somehow or other, both news producer and news reader are able to "make" the news with just the everyday, common-sense knowledge available to them. The news reader in particular is, and must be, able to "find" the news anew each day, with just the newspaper at hand, and with whatever everyday knowledge of the world s/he brings to the task (Hester and Eglin 1997c: 35–38). If members have methods for "seeing" the news in the print, then presumably these methods are available for recovery, inspection, and analysis by members who, for the purpose of doing ethnomethodological studies, put on the special theoretical attitude of the scientist. To adopt the *theoretical attitude* of the inquiring

scientist in order to make the everyday world as seen through the *natural attitude* strange—and thus available for analysis—is not, however, the same as working from, or towards, any particular *theory* of the social world, including a theory of the media. For the point of ethnomethodological studies is to recover the relevancies that the *members* bring to their everyday activities, and not to substitute for them the theory-driven relevancies of the professional sociological inquirer.

4 Early summary accounts are provided by Speier (1970, 1973). See also the very useful summary in Appendix One of Jayyusi (1984).

▼
CHAPTER 2

1 We examine this study of Sacks's in more detail in chapter 4, where it is the model for our inquiry into the rationality of Marc Lépine's course of action.

▼
CHAPTER 3

1 The incongruity between setting and action is one of the bases for the "contrast structures" that Dorothy Smith identifies in her classic analysis of "Angela's" story of how "K" was becoming mentally ill (Smith 1978).

2 For the details of the subsequent story see Rathjen and Montpetit (1999).

3 Appeals by media commentators to such formulations of social context as "the society in which we live," as a way of accounting for the Montreal Massacre, are examined for their membership categorization-analytic features in chapter 6 (see also Hester and Eglin 1997e).

4 This may be slightly unfair to Victor Malarek, the *Globe and Mail*'s principal reporter of the story, who tried to get the police to release the "suicide letter" but to no avail, and who wrote a "final" story asking questions he claimed were going unanswered by the police (Dec 13 [1]). Moreover, these questions do go to the matter of the extent to which Marc Lepine had planned the murders. Nevertheless, beyond printing this article the newspaper did not pursue the political question.

▼
CHAPTER 4

1 Two notable exceptions here, in the ethnomethodological tradition, which *does* recommend serious attention to naturally occurring accounts of (deviant) action, are Wieder (1974) and Zimmerman and Wieder (1977). In addition, it is quite apparent that the symbolic interactionist studies mentioned above are "reworkable" in the terms of membership categorization analysis, though this will not solve the decontextualized character of the accounts contained in them.

2 Just to be clear, in adopting Sacks's model of analysis for use here, we are not importing the substantive topic on which he developed his model. That is, we are not suggesting for a moment that Marc Lépine was engaged in a "search for help" and had found "no-one to turn to."

3 Consider the strategic reasoning reported in "Palestine bombers were disguised as [ultra-orthodox] Jews...in white shirts and black jackets" (*The Record*, Aug 1, 1997, A7) in light of the following remarks by Jayyusi (1984: 69, 70): "In as much as political beliefs, religious affiliations and the like are revelatory matters, they are thus also matters for concealment....In making publicly and routinely available at a glance what is not conventionally thus available [here, "religious person"] one may be thereby providing for a strong relationship to the revealed category incumbency. It may display and provide for an unequivocal, overriding category incumbency

and affiliation to a set of beliefs and practices: a display, in other words, of what is (or should) [*sic*] *take precedence* in terms of categorial identification. This is not to say that such situated displays of relevance...are not also, in occasioned ways, defeasible. Indeed they are." The ease of defeating the categorization "Jewish terrorist" in favour of "Palestinian terrorist" is suggested by Said (1996: xi): "It was often said by complaining journalists and commentators [on his being invited by the BBC to give the 1993 Reith Lectures] that I was a Palestinian, and that, as everyone knew, was synonymous with violence, fanaticism, the killing of Jews."

4   Again, appeals by media commentators to such formulations of social context as "the society in which we live," as a way of accounting for the Montreal Massacre are examined for their membership categorization-analytic features in chapter 6 (see also Hester and Eglin 1997e).

5   We are modelling this analysis of denunciation/denounceable on Turner's (1976) analysis of complaint/complainable.

6   Their caution may well have been justified: "They were horrified when Alice de Wolff, a Toronto organizer for the National Action Committee on the Status of Women, told them that among all the calls the organization's Ottawa office received yesterday from women across Canada, there was a threatening one from an angry man who told them 'that Marc is not alone'" (Dec 8 [7]). "As police watched over the Victoria event [a vigil], organizer Mariane Alto told the crowd a man had telephoned her to say he felt the job in Montreal wasn't finished and he would be at the vigil" (*KWR*, Dec 11 [1]).

7   See Susan Donaldson and Will Kymlicka (Analysis), "No thaw in chilly campus climate," the *Globe and Mail*, November 17, 1989, A8.

8   Spider Robinson (1997) poses the same formal dilemma with respect to the political task of opposing the Multilateral Agreement on Investment (MAI). The agency one would appeal to in order to stop the agreement, namely the government, is the agency bringing it into existence. In this case there is the additional twist that when in place the agreement would effectively dismantle government in favour of business, so removing the possibility of democratically peaceful opposition. "Has anyone out there a suggestion?" he writes. "All that occurs to me are armed insurrection or terrorism."

9   We wish to acknowledge and thank Jeannette Gaudet (French and Gender Studies, St. Thomas University, New Brunswick) for drawing our attention to the significance of the last major paragraph in the letter. When Eglin presented a version of this chapter at the Discourse Analysis Research Group second annual one-day conference on "Gender and Discourse/Theory and Discourse" at St. Thomas University on March 28, 1998, Dr. Gaudet kindly pointed out how the Olympic Games, the Canadian armed forces, and Caesar's legions were, traditionally, all-male preserves.

10 Let us enter a note of caution here. We are, of course, not seeking to justify Lépine's abominable actions. Indeed, to engage in such an enterprise would be to risk, as Chomsky said of debating the Holocaust, losing one's humanity. Suffice it to say that there is no evidence Lépine engaged the democratic process, let alone exhausted its possibilities. His arguments, such as they are, are factually wrong or tendentious, and easily countered. And terrorism, in our view, whether of the wholesale kind carried out by governments or the retail kind done by individuals or groups (Chomsky and Herman 1979) trashes human rights and cannot be justified (nor, in this case, excused). Our point, however, is to focus on the rhetorical structure of Lépine's reasoning, and to show how it could lead him to the murderous course of action he undertook. We take up the ethical issues such a methodological strategy may nevertheless pose in the last chapter.

11 It later became known that Lépine had applied for admission that fall to the Polytechnique, but had been rejected.

12 The same frame of interpretation is reproduced in at least three academic textbook
treatments of murder. Thus, in the chapter on murder in his textbook on crime and
deviance in Canada, Ian Gomme (1998) arranges his discussion in terms of different
types of murder. Under the title "Hunting Humans" he distinguishes the sub-types
of "serial killing" and "mass murder"; the Montreal Massacre is included under the
latter category (224–225). His next major category of murder, beginning on the next
page, is "terrorism." Though the Front de Libération du Québec's (FLQ) kidnapping
and murder of Pierre Laporte finds its place here, there is no mention of Denis Lortie or Marc Lépine. Similarly, James Fox and Jack Levin (2001) put Marc Lépine in their
chapter on mass murder (titled "Rampage," 119) rather than in the following chapter on hate homicides (which includes domestic terrorism). Finally, though Thomas
O'Reilly-Fleming's (1996) collection *Serial and Mass Murder: Theory, Research and Policy* is peppered with mentions of the Montreal Massacre, and dedicated to its victims,
analysis of the event extends no further than it being classified (15–16) as mass murder (as opposed to serial murder), and to this remark: "Because we do not understand
or agree with the motives of the Montreal killer of 6 December 1989, it does not make
this crime any less motivated" (Dietz, in O'Reilly-Fleming, 114).

▼
CHAPTER 5

1 Recalling the discussion of "character appears on cue" from chapter 2, we note again
but will not topicalize further here the categorial order pertaining to the kinds of
commentary and the category membership of the various commentators. Thus, it
is unsurprising that the parties providing commentary should provide the kind of
commentary that they do in fact make. Furthermore, it is again quite unremarkable
that such categories of person should be selected by news media for their particular contributions.

2 As we indicated in summary form in note 2 of chapter 1, our findings do not support
the claim of the publisher of Malette and Chalouh (1991: [9]) that "the mainstream
media scrambled to ignore or downplay the significance of the victims being women"
and that "the analysis of feminists was ignored or ridiculed or rejected with hostility," nor that of Bart and Moran (1993: xiii) that "although the Montreal killer said that
he murdered the women because he hated feminists, the debate that followed attributed his behavior simply to psychopathology, ignoring the fact that he was a woman-
hating man reinforced by a woman-hating society" (cited in Meyers 1997: 11), nor
that of Meyers herself that "the news ignored feminist expertise on male violence"
(1997: 11), nor even that of Mahood (1996: 367) that "the initial press coverage
described Lépine's violence as the isolated actions of a madman"—the *Globe and
Mail*, at least, certainly did make and report such descriptions in the initial news coverage, as we said in chapter 4, but other, feminist-type descriptions were made and
reported as well, as we have shown in the first part of the current chapter. That is, at
least in our materials, the feminist analysis of the massacre as the product of
"a woman-hating man reinforced by a woman-hating society" became the paramount frame of interpretation in the news *commentaries* on the events (as we sig-
nalled in chapter 1). We might also point out that this reference to Bart and Moran's
work, plus an accompanying reference to Malette and Chalouh (1991) on the same
page, constitute the entire treatment of news coverage of the Montreal Massacre in
Meyers's book, entitled *News Coverage of Violence against Women*. Furthermore, in
Bart and Moran's (1993) edited collection, *Violence against Women: The Bloody Foot-*

prints, the passage cited by Meyers and repeated by us above, and a two-page report by Stato (1993), are all that contributors to that work have to say about the massacre. In *Social Control in Canada: Issues in the Social Construction of Deviance* (Schissel and Mahood 1996) Mahood's two paragraphs, and two sentences in Adam (1996: 237), are all there is. Of the forty-two contributions (not counting section introductions) to *Femicide: The Politics of Woman Killing* (Radford and Russell 1992) one only (to the extent of four paragraphs) concerns itself with the Montreal Massacre (Caputi and Russell 1992), while Radford includes mention of it in her introduction to the book (Radford 1992: 5–6) and Russell, in her preface, cites its importance as "ma[king] the existence of the phenomenon of femicide, at least for some, impossible to ignore" (Russell 1992: xv). In their textbook *Woman Abuse: A Sociological Story* DeKeseredy and MacLeod (1997: 164, 139) devote one paragraph and part of one sentence to it, while Marilyn French gives it a paragraph in *The War against Women* (1992: 196). The topic does not appear at all in Holly Johnson's *Dangerous Domains: Violence against Women in Canada* (1996) nor in the large recent collection *Sourcebook on Violence against Women* (Renzetti, Edleson, and Bergen 2001). Given its perceived importance, indeed its perhaps unique status, it is curious how little sustained analysis—certainly nothing of book-length—of the Massacre has appeared to date.

3 The condemnatory and hence moral-political character of these categorizations in the commentaries constituted the paramount context for engagement with the Montreal Massacre. It is with reference to this moral-political context, provided by the phenomenon under investigation, that our own responses were shaped. We were "captured" by this context and found its auspices seductive. We address these matters in our conclusion.

4 See Sacks (1974) and Hester (1998) on some other examples of the use of positioned category devices. For the professional, social-scientific, feminist version of the "pranks-through-to-violence" continuum, consider the following: "Femicide is on the extreme end of a continuum of antifemale terror that includes a wide variety of verbal and physical abuse, such as rape, torture, sexual slavery (particularly in prostitution), incestuous and extrafamilial child sexual abuse, physical and emotional battery, sexual harassment (on the phone, in the streets, at the office, and in the classroom), genital mutilation (clitoridectomies, excision, infibulation), unnecessary gynecological operations (gratuitous hysterectomies), forced heterosexuality, forced sterilization, forced motherhood (by criminalizing contraception and abortion), psychosurgery, denial of food to women in some cultures, cosmetic surgery, and other mutilations in the name of beautification. Whenever these forms of terrorism result in death, they become femicides" (Caputi and Russell 1992: 15).

5 It may be further noted that in formulating the difference between the feminist and non-feminist versions of the significance of the murders as one between two *opposing* sides, the debate format or contrast class invites the reader to take one side or the other. As we suggest in our conclusion, it is easy then for any reader, including analysts, to get drawn into this morality play; and it is then not surprising when one who attempts to resist such incorporation has their resistance treated as itself an instance of their participation in it.

CHAPTER 6

1 Compare Coulter's (1989) discussion of the operational relevance of categories, and recall Garfinkel (1967: 31): "a common understanding, entailing as it does an 'inner' temporal course of interpretive work, necessarily has an operational structure."

2   The examples that Drew and Heritage cite nevertheless tend to impose contexts.

3   This combined personal-and-sociological category analysis of the Massacre is repeated in the professional literature. Meyers (1997: 11), for example, writes as follows: "Bart and Moran (1993), although noting that the vast majority of mass murderers are men and their victims most often women, agree that a man who commits mass murder is 'deranged.' But they point out that 'his choice of victims also reflects the misogyny being supported in the culture' (79)." Bart and Moran do not refer explicitly to the Montreal Massacre in this passage, however.

4   Theodore Sasson (1995: 87ff) discovers other members articulating, like Valpy in "Litany of social ills," the theme of "blocked opportunities" as one among a small number of explanatory frames used to account for crime. He identifies the social scientific roots of this construct in Merton's 1938 essay on "Social Structure and Anomie." But he appears to treat members' formulations of this argument as popular derivations of the professional sociologist's theory, rather than seeing Merton's account as being thoroughly grounded in and dependent on members' methods for using social structure.

▼
CHAPTER 7

1   Indeed, in this regard ambiguities in earlier functionalist formulations of this argument were cleared up by, for example, Roshier (1977; see also Box 1981: 36–40). Thus, in earlier formulations it could have been understood that what was being referred to was the objective character of crime, not its interpreted character.

▼
CHAPTER 8

1   The emergence of critical inquiry into the sociological and criminological mainstream may be less subversive of the status quo than it appears. For one thing, it perpetuates the long-held traditional view that it is the analyst who knows best, that it is he or she who has a better view of the nature of things than the mere commonsense member of society. Whether the point of inquiry is inequality, the removal of oppression, or the furtherance of human rights, the stance and the logic remains the same: the analyst speaks from a privileged viewpoint; it is he or she who may teach and instruct those who do not know any better.

2   It is instructive that when members of the audience objected, they did so as category incumbents. Moreover, they elected incumbency, not in terms of the setting-generated category of "sociologist," but as "feminists" or "oppressed women." It was these membership categories that were invoked and that provided for their objection. And it is indeed unsurprising that such an objection would be made insofar as a predicate of the category feminist is the engagement in pro-women actions. That is, as incumbents of these categories—oppressed women, feminists—certain activities are implied and made relevant. These include responding in particular ways. So, identifying with Lépine's victims and expressing outrage with the re-presentation of his crime may be said to be category-tied activities of these self-categorizations.

3   Such a separation of ethnomethodology and politics does not, of course, mean that the erstwhile ethnomethodologist may not take up political questions in contexts other than those of ethnomethodological inquiry. Indeed, one of us (Eglin 1998/99) has become increasingly involved in precisely such questions, including those of "being a man" and being a political actor posed by Marc Lépine's murderous actions in Montreal (Eglin forthcoming: chap. 3). This has necessarily involved a shift in analytic orientation.

4 See Jefferson (1984) for an insightful analysis of some sequential organizational features of news receipt.
5 The political effectiveness of *any* form of sociological inquiry is questionable in this regard.

References

Adam, B. (1996). Constructing Sexuality in the AIDS Era. In B. Schissel and L. Mahood (Eds.), *Social Control in Canada: A Reader in the Social Construction of Deviance*. Toronto, ON: Oxford University Press. 227–240.

Anderson, D.G. and Sharrock, W.W. (1979). Biasing the News: Technical Issues in "Media Studies." *Sociology* 13 (3): 367–385.

Athens, L. (1980). *Violent Criminal Acts and Actors*. London, UK: Routledge and Kegan Paul.

Atkinson, J.M. (1978). *Discovering Suicide: Studies in the Social Organization of Sudden Death*. London, UK: Macmillan.

Atkinson, M.A. (1980). Some Practical Uses of a "Natural Lifetime." *Human Studies* 3 (1): 33–46.

Austin, J.L. (1962). *How to Do Things with Words*. Oxford, UK: Clarendon.

Bart, P.B. and Moran, E.G. (Eds.) (1993). *Violence against Women: The Bloody Footprints*. A Gender and Society Reader. Newbury Park, CA: Sage.

Becker, H.D. (1963). *Outsiders: Studies in the Sociology of Deviance*. New York, NY: Free Press.

Best, J. (Ed.) (1995). *Images of Issues: Typifying Contemporary Social Problems*. Second edition. Hawthorne, NY: Aldine de Gruyter.

Blum, A. and McHugh, P. (1971). The Social Ascription of Motives. *American Sociological Review* 36: 98–109.

Bogen, D. and Lynch, M. (1993). Do We Need a General Theory of Social Problems? In J. Holstein and G. Miller (Eds.), *Reconsidering Social Constructionism*. Hawthorne, NY: Aldine de Gruyter. 83–107.

Box, S. (1981 [1971]). *Deviance, Reality and Society*. Second edition. London, UK: Holt, Rinehart and Winston.

Button, G. (Ed.) (1991). *Ethnomethodology and the Human Sciences*. Cambridge, UK: Cambridge University Press.

Caputi, J. and Russell, D.E.H. (1992). Femicide: Sexist Terrorism against Women. In J. Radford and D.E.H. Russell (Eds.) *Femicide: The Politics of Woman Killing*. New York, NY: Twayne. 13–21. (Earlier version published as "Femicide": Speaking the Unspeakable in *Ms.* (September/October 1990): 34–37.)

Chomsky, N. (1996). *Class Warfare*. Interviews with David Barsamian. Monroe, ME: Common Courage Press.

Chomsky, N. and Herman, E. (1979). *The Political Economy of Human Rights.* Two volumes. Montreal, QC: Black Rose.

Cicourel, A.V. (1964). *Method and Measurement in Sociology.* New York, NY: Free Press.

Coulter, J. (1974). The Ethnomethodological Programme in Contemporary Sociology. *The Human Context* 6 (1): 103–122.

Coulter, J. (1982). Remarks on the Conceptualization of Social Structure. *Philosophy of the Social Sciences* 12 (1): 33–46.

Coulter, J. (1989). *Mind in Action.* Oxford, UK: Polity Press.

Coulter, J. (Ed.) (1990). *Ethnomethodological Sociology.* Schools of Thought in Sociology 2. Aldershot, UK: Edward Elgar.

Cressey, D. (1953). *Other People's Money.* Glencoe, IL: Free Press.

Cuff, E.C. (1994). *Problems of Versions in Everyday Situations.* Washington, DC: University Press of America and the International Institute for Ethnomethodology and Conversation Analysis.

Cuff, E.C., Francis, D. and Sharrock, W.W. (1990). *Perspectives in Sociology.* Third edition. London, UK: Routledge.

DeKeseredy, W. and MacLeod, L. (1997). *Woman Abuse: A Sociological Study.* Toronto, ON: Harcourt Brace Canada.

Dietz, M.L. (1996). Killing Sequentially: Expanding the Parameters of the Conceptualization of Serial and Mass Killers. In T. O'Reilly-Fleming (Ed.), *Serial and Mass Murder: Theory, Research and Policy.* Toronto, ON: Canadian Scholars' Press. 109–120.

Drew, P. (1978). Accusations: the Occasioned Use of Members' Knowledge of "Religious Geography" in Describing Events. *Sociology* 12 (1): 1–22.

Drew, P. and Heritage, J. (1992). Analyzing Talk at Work: An Introduction. In P. Drew and J. Heritage (Eds.), *Talk at Work: Interaction in Institutional Settings.* Cambridge, UK: Cambridge University Press. 3–65.

Durkheim, E. (1951 [1897]). *Suicide: A Study in Sociology.* New York, NY: Free Press.

Durkheim, E. (1982 [1895]). *The Rules of Sociological Method.* Chicago, IL: University of Chicago Press.

Eglin, P. (1979a). How Conversational Analysis Elucidates Schutz's Common-sense Concept of Rationality. *Sociolinguistics Newsletter* 10 (2): 11–17.

Eglin, P. (1979b). Resolving Reality Disjunctures on Telegraph Avenue: A Study of Practical Reasoning. *Canadian Journal of Sociology* 4 (4): 359–377.

Eglin, P. (1985). *Suicide.* Teaching Papers in Sociology. York, UK: Longman.

Eglin, P. (1998/99). Partnership in an Evil Action: Canadian Universities, Indonesia and Genocide in East Timor. *Brock Review* 7 (1/2): 57–99.

Eglin, P. (forthcoming). Pin-up, Panty Raid and Massacre: Being a Man. Chapter 3 in *Getting a Life: A Story of Studies in Pursuit of Intellectual Responsibility.*

Eglin, P. and Hester, S. (1992). Category, Predicate and Task: The Pragmatics of Practical Action. *Semiotica* 88: 243–268.

Eglin, P. and Hester, S. (1999a). Moral Order and the Montreal Massacre: A Story of Membership Categorization Analysis. In P. Jalbert (Ed.), *Media Studies: Ethnomethodological Approaches.* Lanham, MD: University Press of America, and the International Institute for Ethnomethodology and Conversation Analysis. 195–230.

Eglin, P. and Hester, S. (1999b). "You're All a Bunch of Feminists": Categorization and the Politics of Terror. *Human Studies* 22 (2–4): 253–272.

Fahmy, P. (Ed.) (1994). *Feminist Perspective: The Events of Polytechnique—Analyses and Proposals for Action*. Trans. G. Landry. Ottawa, ON: Canadian Research Institute for the Advancement of Women.

Ferrell, J. and Websdale, N. (Eds.) (1999). *Making Trouble: Cultural Constructions of Crime, Deviance, and Control*. Hawthorne, NY: Aldine de Gruyter.

Fishman, M. (1980). *Manufacturing the News*. Austin and London: University of Texas Press.

Fox, J.A. and Levin, J. (2001). *The Will to Kill: Making Sense of Senseless Murder*. Toronto, ON: Allyn and Bacon.

French, M. (1992). *The War against Women*. New York, NY: Summit Books.

Garfinkel, H. (1967). *Studies in Ethnomethodology*. Englewood Cliffs, NJ: Prentice-Hall.

Garfinkel, H. (1991). Respecification: Evidence for Locally Produced, Naturally Accountable Phenomena of Order, Logic, Reason, Meaning, Method, etc. in and as of the Essential Haecceity of Immortal Ordinary Society (I)—An Announcement of Studies. In G. Button (Ed.), *Ethnomethodology and the Human Sciences*. Cambridge, UK: Cambridge University Press. 10–19.

Garfinkel, H. and Sacks, H. (1970). On Formal Structures of Practical Actions. In J.C. McKinney and E.A. Tiryakian (Eds.), *Theoretical Sociology: Perspectives and Developments*. New York, NY: Appleton-Century-Crofts. 337–366. (Reprinted in H. Garfinkel (Ed.) (1986) *Ethnomethodological Studies of Work*. London, UK: Routledge and Kegan Paul; and in Coulter [1990].)

Gomme, I. (1998). *The Shadow Line: Deviance and Crime in Canada*. Second edition. Toronto, ON: Harcourt Brace, Canada.

Grusky, O. and Pollner, M. (Eds.) (1981). *The Sociology of Mental Illness: Basic Readings*. New York, NY: Holt, Rinehart and Winston.

Gusfield, J. (1981). *The Culture of Public Problems: Drinking Driving and the Symbolic Order*. Chicago, IL: Chicago University Press.

Gusfield, J. (1989). Constructing the Ownership of Social Problems: Fun and Profit in the Welfare State. *Social Problems* 36 (5): 431–441.

Habermas, J. (1972). *Knowledge and Human Interests*. Trans. J.J. Shapiro. London, UK: Heinemann.

Hagan, J. and Leon, J. (1977). Rediscovering Delinquency: Social History, Political Ideology and the Sociology of Law. *American Sociological Review* 42: 587–598.

Henry, A.F. and Short, J.F. (1954). *Suicide and Homicide: Some Economic, Sociological, and Psychological Aspects of Aggression*. Glencoe, IL: Free Press.

Heritage, J. (1985). Analyzing News Interviews: Aspects of the Production of Talk for an Overhearing Audience. In T. van Dijk (Ed.), *Handbook of Discourse Analysis*, Vol. 3: *Discourse and Dialogue*. London, UK: Academic Press. 95–117.

Heritage, J. and Watson, D.R. (1979). Formulations as Conversational Objects. In G. Psathas (Ed.), *Everyday Language: Studies in Ethnomethodology*. New York, NY: Irvington. 123–162.

Hester, S. (1989). The Social Organization of Contrast and Complementarity in Assessments. Paper presented at the International Institute for Ethnomethodology and Conversation Analysis Conference, Boston University (Andover).

Hester, S. (1990). The Social Facts of Deviance in School: A Study of Mundane Reason. *British Journal of Sociology* 42 (3): 443–463.

Hester, S. (1992). Recognizing References to Deviance in Referral Talk. In G. Watson and R.M. Seiler (Eds.), *Text in Context: Contributions to Ethnomethodology*. Newbury Park, CA: Sage. 156–174.

Hester, S. (1998). Describing Deviance in School: Recognizably Educational Psychological Problems. In C. Antaki and S. Widdicombe (Eds.), *Identities in Talk*. London, UK: Sage. 133–150.

Hester, S. and Eglin, P. (1992). *A Sociology of Crime*. London: Routledge.

Hester, S. and Eglin, P. (Eds.) (1997a). *Culture in Action: Studies in Membership Categorization Analysis*. Washington, DC: University Press of America and International Institute for Ethnomethodology and Conversation Analysis.

Hester, S. and Eglin, P. (1997b). Membership Categorization Analysis: An Introduction. In S. Hester and P. Eglin (Eds.), *Culture in Action: Studies in Membership Categorization Analysis*. Washington, DC: University Press of America and International Institute for Ethnomethodology and Conversation Analysis. 1–23.

Hester, S. and Eglin, P. (1997c). The Reflexive Constitution of Category, Predicate and Context in Two Settings. In S. Hester and P. Eglin (Eds.), *Culture in Action: Studies in Membership Categorization Analysis*. Washington, DC: University Press of America and International Institute for Ethnomethodology and Conversation Analysis. 25–48.

Hester, S. and Eglin, P. (1997d). Conclusion: Membership Categorization Analysis and Sociology. In S. Hester and P. Eglin (Eds.), *Culture in Action: Studies in Membership Categorization Analysis*. Washington, DC: University Press of America and International Institute for Ethnomethodology and Conversation Analysis. 153–163.

Hester, S. and Eglin, P. (1997e). Accounting for the Montreal Massacre: Re–specifying Professional and Lay Sociological Accounting Practices as Membership Categorization Analysis. Paper presented at the 14th Annual Qualitative Research Conference, Ontario Institute for Studies in Education, University of Toronto, August 8.

Hester, S. and Francis, D. (1997). Reality Analysis in a Classroom Storytelling. *British Journal of Sociology* 48 (1): 95–112.

Hester, S. and Francis, D. (2000). Ethnomethodology, Conversation Analysis and "Institutional Talk." *Text* 20 (3): 373–413.

Holstein, J. and Miller, G. (Eds.) (1993). *Reconsidering Social Constructionism*. Hawthorne, NY: Aldine de Gruyter.

Jalbert, P. (Ed.) (1999). *Media Studies: Ethnomethodological Approaches*. Lanham, MD: University Press of America, and International Institute for Ethnomethodology and Conversation Analysis.

Jayyusi, L. (1984). *Categorization and the Moral Order*. London, UK: Routledge and Kegan Paul.

Jefferson, G. (1984). Notes on a Systematic Deployment of the Acknowledgement Tokens "Yeah" and "mm hm." *Papers in Linguistics* 17 (2): 197–216.

Jenkins, P. (1994). *Using Murder: The Social Construction of Serial Homicide*. Hawthorne, NY: Aldine de Gruyter.

Johnson, H. (1996). *Dangerous Domains: Violence against Women in Canada*. Scarborough, ON: Nelson Canada.

Johnson, J. (1981). Program Enterprise and Official Cooptation in the Battered Women's Shelter Movement. *American Behavioral Scientist* 24 (6): 827–842.

Johnson, J. (1995). Horror Stories and the Construction of Child Abuse. In J. Best (Ed.), *Images of Issues: Typifying Contemporary Social Problems*. Second edition. Hawthorne, NY: Aldine de Gruyter. 17–31.

Junas, D. (1995). The Rise of Citizen Militias: Angry White Guys with Guns. *Covert Action Quarterly*, 52 (Spring).

Kleck, G, and Sayles, S. (1990). Rape and Resistance. *Social Problems* 37 (2): 149–162.

Lee, J.R.E. (1984). Innocent Victims and Evil Doers. *Women's Studies International Forum* 7: 69–78.

Leyton, E. (1992). The Theatre of Public Crisis. In E. Leyton, W. O'Grady and J. Overton, *Violence and Public Anxiety*. St. John's, NL: Institute of Social and Economic Research. 109–191.

Loseke, D. (1992). *The Battered Woman and Shelters: The Social Construction of Wife Abuse*. Albany, NY: State University of New York Press.

Loseke, D. (1999). *Thinking about Social Problems: An Introduction to Constructionist Perspectives*. Hawthorne, NY: Aldine de Gruyter.

Lynch, M. (1993). *Scientific Practice and Ordinary Action: Ethnomethodology and Social Studies of Science*. New York, NY: Cambridge University Press.

Mahood, L. (1996). Campus Sex Crime, Journalism and Social Control. In B. Schissel and L. Mahood (Eds.), *Social Control in Canada: A Reader in the Social Construction of Deviance*. Toronto, ON: Oxford University Press. 352–372.

Malette, L. and Chalouh, M. (Eds.) (1991). *The Montreal Massacre*. Trans. M. Wildeman. Charlottetown, PEI: Gynergy Books.

Matza, D. (1964). *Delinquency and Drift*. New York: Wiley.

Maynard, D. (1988). Language, Interaction and Social Problems. *Social Problems* 35 (4): 311–334.

McCormack, T. (1990). Questions in the Aftermath: Engineering Feminism. *This Magazine*, 24 (1): 31–32.

McCormick, C. (1995). *The (Mis-)Representation of Crime in the News*. Halifax, NS: Fernwood.

McHoul, A. and Watson, D. R. (1984). Two Axes for the Analysis of "Commonsense" and "Formal" Geographical Knowledge in the Classroom. *British Journal of the Sociology of Education* 5 (3): 281–302.

Merton, R.K. (1938). Social Structure and Anomie. *American Sociological Review* 3: 672–682.

Meyers, M. (1997). *News Coverage of Violence against Women: Engendering Blame*. Thousand Oaks, CA: Sage.

Miller, G. and Holstein, J. (Eds.) (1993). *Constructionist Controversies*. Hawthorne, NY: Aldine de Gruyter.

O'Reilly-Fleming, T. (Ed.) (1996). *Serial and Mass Murder: Theory, Research and Policy*. Toronto, ON: Canadian Scholars' Press.

Pfohl, S. (1977). The "Discovery" of Child Abuse. *Social Problems* 24 (3): 310–323.

Pollner, M. (1974a). Mundane Reasoning. *Philosophy of the Social Sciences* 4: 35–54.

Pollner, M. (1974b). Sociological and Common-sense Models of the Labelling Process. In R. Turner (Ed.), *Ethnomethodology: Selected Readings*. Harmondsworth, UK: Penguin. 27–40.

Pollner, M. (1978). Constitutive and Mundane Versions of Labelling Theory. *Human Studies* 1: 269–288.

Pollner, M. (1987). *Mundane Reason: Reality in Everyday and Sociological Discourse.* Cambridge, UK: Cambridge University Press.

Potter, G. and Kappeler, V. (Eds.) (1998). *Constructing Crime: Perspectives on Making News and Social Problems.* Prospect Heights, IL: Waveland.

Radford, J. (1992). Introduction. In J. Radford and D.E.H. Russell (Eds.) *Femicide: The Politics of Woman Killing.* New York, NY: Twayne. 3–12.

Radford, J. and Russell, D.E.H. (Eds.) (1992). *Femicide: The Politics of Woman Killing.* New York, NY: Twayne.

Rathjen, H. and Montpetit, C. (1999). *December 6: From the Montreal Massacre to Gun Control: The Inside Story.* Toronto, ON: McClelland and Stewart.

Renzetti, C. M., Edleson, J.L. and Bergen, R.K. (Eds.) 2001. *Sourcebook on Violence against Women.* Thousand Oaks, CA: Sage.

Robinson, S. (1997). The Scent of a Done Deal. The *Globe and Mail*, August 4, A11.

Roshier, R. (1977). The Functions of Crime Myth. *Sociological Review* 25: 309–324.

Rubington, E. and Weinberg, M. (Eds.) (1987). *Deviance: The Interactionist Perspective.* Fifth edition. New York, NY: Macmillan.

Russell, D.E.H. (1992). Preface. In J. Radford and D.E.H. Russell (Eds.) *Femicide: The Politics of Woman Killing.* New York, NY: Twayne Publishers. xiv–xv.

Sacks, H. (1963). Sociological Description. *Berkeley Journal of Sociology* 8 (1): 1–16.

Sacks, H. (1967). The Search for Help: No One to Turn To. In E. Shneidman (Ed.), *Essays in Self Destruction.* New York, NY: Science House. 202–223.

Sacks, H. (1972). An Initial Investigation of the Usability of Conversational Data for Doing Sociology. In D. Sudnow (Ed.), *Studies in Social Interaction.* New York: Free Press. 31–74.

Sacks, H. (1974). On the Analyzability of Stories by Children. In R. Turner (Ed.), *Ethnomethodology: Selected Readings.* Harmondsworth, UK: Penguin Books. 216–232.

Sacks, H. (1979). Hotrodder: A Revolutionary Category. In G. Psathas (Ed.), *Everyday Language: Studies in Ethnomethodology.* New York, NY: Irvington. 7–14.

Sacks, H. (1986). Some Considerations of a Story Told in Ordinary Conversation. *Poetics* 15: 127–38.

Sacks, H. (1992a). *Lectures on Conversation, Volume One.* Oxford, UK: Basil Blackwell.

Sacks, H. (1992b). *Lectures on Conversation, Volume Two.* Oxford, UK: Basil Blackwell.

Said, E.W. (1994). *Culture and Imperialism.* New York, NY: Vintage.

Said, E.W. (1996). *Representations of the Intellectual.* The 1993 Reith Lectures. New York, NY: Vintage.

Salutin, R. (1997). When Politics Doesn't Do Much for You, There's Always Crime. The *Globe and Mail*, August 8, C1.

Sasson, S. (1995). *Crime Talk: How Citizens Construct a Social Problem.* Hawthorne, NY: Aldine de Gruyter.

Schegloff, E. (1972). Notes on a Conversational Practice: Formulating Place. In D. Sudnow (Ed.), *Studies in Social Interaction*. New York, NY: Free Press. 75–119.

Schegloff, E. (1991). Reflections on Talk and Social Structure. In D. Boden and D. Zimmerman (Eds.), *Talk and Social Structure: Studies in Ethnomethodology and Conversation Analysis*. Cambridge, UK: Polity Press. 44–70.

Schissel, B. and Mahood, L. (Eds.) (1996). *Social Control in Canada: A Reader on the Social Construction of Deviance*. Toronto, ON: Oxford University Press.

Scott, M. and Lyman, S. (1970). Accounts, Deviance and Social Order. In J. Douglas (Ed.), *Deviance and Respectability: The Social Construction of Moral Meanings*. New York, NY: Basic Books. 89–119.

Sharrock, W.W. (1974). On Owning Knowledge. In R. Turner (Ed.), *Ethnomethodology: Selected Readings*. Harmondsworth, UK: Penguin. 45–53.

Sharrock, W.W. (1984). The Social Realities of Deviance. In R.J. Anderson and W.W. Sharrock (Eds.), *Applied Perspectives in Sociology*. London, UK: George Allen and Unwin. 86–105.

Sharrock, W. W. and Button, G. (1991). The Social Actor: Social Action in Real Time. In G. Button (Ed.), *Ethnomethodology and the Human Sciences*. Cambridge, UK: Cambridge University Press. 137–175.

Sharrock, W.W. and Watson, D.R. (1988). Autonomy among Social Theories: The Incarnation of Social Structures. In N. Fielding (Ed.), *Actions and Structure: Research Methods and Social Theory*. London, UK: Sage.

Sharrock, W.W. and Watson, D.R. (1989). Talk and Police Work: Notes on the Traffic in Information. In H. Coleman (Ed.), *Working with Language: A Multidisciplinary Consideration of Language Use in Work Contexts*. Berlin and New York: Mouton de Gruyter.

Smith, D.E. (1975). The Statistics on Mental Illness: (What They Do Not Tell Us about Women and Why). In D. Smith and S.J. David (Eds.), *Women Look at Psychiatry*. Vancouver, BC: Press Gang. 73–119.

Smith, D.E. (1978). "K is Mentally Ill:" The Anatomy of a Factual Account. *Sociology* 12: 23–53.

Smith, D.E. (1992). Whistling Women: Rage and Rationality. In W.K. Carroll, L. Christiansen-Ruffman, R.F. Currie, and D. Harrison (Eds.), *Fragile Truths: 25 Years of Sociology and Anthropology in Canada*. Ottawa, ON: Carleton University Press. 207–226.

Spector, M. and Kitsuse, J.I. (1987 [1977]). *Constructing Social Problems*. Hawthorne, NY: Aldine de Gruyter.

Speier, M. (1970). The Everyday World of the Child. In J.D. Douglas (Ed.), *Understanding Everyday Life: Toward the Reconstruction of Sociological Knowledge*. Chicago, IL: Aldine. 188–218.

Speier, M. (1973). *How To Observe Face-to-Face Communication: A Sociological Introduction*. Pacific Palisades, CA: Goodyear.

Stato, J. (1993). Montreal Gynocide. In P.B. Bart and E.G. Moran (Eds.), *Violence against Women: The Bloody Footprints*. Newbury Park, CA: Sage. 132–133.

Tierney, K. (1982). The Battered Women Movement and the Creation of the Wife Beating Problem. *Social Problems* 29 (3): 207–220.

Turner, Roy. (1970). Words, Utterances and Activities. In J.D. Douglas (Ed.), *Understanding Everyday Life: Toward the Reconstruction of Sociological Knowledge.* Chicago, IL: Aldine. 169–187.

Turner, Roy. (1976). Utterance Positioning as an Interactional Resource. *Semiotica* 17: 233–254.

United Nations (1986 [1948]). *The Universal Declaration of Human Rights.* New York, NY: United Nations Department of Public Information.

Watson, D.R. (1978). Categorization, Authorization and Blame–Negotiation. *Sociology* 12: 105–113.

Watson, D.R. (1983). The Presentation of "Victim" and "Motive" in Discourse: The Case of Police Interrogations and Interviews. *Victimology: An International Journal* 8 (1/2): 31–52.

Watson, D.R. (1990). Some Features of the Elicitation of Confessions in Murder Interrogations. In G. Psathas (Ed.), *Interaction Competence.* Washington, DC: University Press of America and International Institute for Ethnomethodology and Conversation Analysis. 263–295.

Wieder, D.L. (1974). *Language and Social Reality: The Case of Telling the Convict Code.* The Hague, NL: Mouton.

Wittgenstein, L. (1958). *Philosophical Investigations.* Oxford, UK: Basil Blackwell.

Wowk, M. (1984). Blame Allocation, Sex and Gender in a Murder Interrogation. *Women's Studies International Forum* 7: 75–82.

Zimmerman, D. and Pollner, M. (1971). The Everyday World as a Phenomenon. In J.D. Douglas (Ed.), *Understanding Everyday Life: Towards the Reconstruction of Sociological Knowledge.* London, UK: Routledge and Kegan Paul. 80–103.

Zimmerman, D. and Wieder, D.L. (1977). "You Can't Help But Get Stoned": Notes on the Social Organization of Marijuana Smoking. *Social Problems* 25: 198–207.

Index